A Dreac

or, A Young Wife's Ambition

Mrs. Alex. McVeigh Miller

Alpha Editions

This edition published in 2021

ISBN : 9789355345622

Design and Setting By
Alpha Editions
www.alphaedis.com
Email - info@alphaedis.com

Contents

CHAPTER I.

"Hear the mellow wedding-bells—
Golden bells!
What a world of happiness
Their melody foretells!"

"Hark! there's the wedding-march."

"Here they come!"

"Looks as white as a corpse, doesn't she?"

"Oh, no; as beautiful as a dream, to my notion. Pallor is becoming in brides, you know."

"He's a silly old dotard, though, not to know that she's taking him for his money."

"Of course he knows it. I dare say the old gray-beard is glad he had money enough to buy so much youth and loveliness."

"What a splendid veil and dress! They say her rich aunt furnished the *trousseau.*"

"Her jewels are magnificent."

"The bridegroom's gift, of course. Well, he is able to cover her with diamonds."

These were but few of the remarks that were whispered in the fashionable throng gathered at Trinity to witness a marriage in high life—a marriage that was all the more interesting from the fact that the contracting parties were so totally dissimilar to each other that the whole affair in the eyes of the outsiders resolved itself into a simple matter of bargain and sale—so much youth and beauty for an old man's gold.

The bridegroom was John St. John, a millionaire of high birth and standing in the city where he lived, but so old and infirm that people said of him that "he had one foot in the grave and the other on the brink of it," and the bride was the young daughter of some obscure country people.

An aunt in the city had given her some advantages, and kept her in town two seasons, hoping to bring about a good match for her, since she had no dowry of her own, save youth, talent and peerless beauty.

"And what is your fortune, my pretty maid?""My face is my fortune, sir," she said.

And Xenie Carroll was fulfilling her aunt's ambitious hopes and desires to their uttermost limit as she walked up the broad aisle of Trinity that night, clothed in her bridal white, and leaning on the arm of the decrepit old millionaire, John St. John.

His form was bent with age, his hair and beard were white, his eyes were dim and bleared; and she was in the bloom of youth and beauty. It was the union of winter and summer.

They passed slowly up the aisle to the grand music of the wedding-march, and after them came fair maidens, robed in white and adorned with flowers and jewels.

These stood round about the pair at the altar who were taking upon their lips the sacred vow of marriage.

It was over.

The holy man of God lifted reverent hands and invoked God's blessing upon this sordid bargain that desecrated the holy rite of marriage, the ring was slipped over the bride's white finger, and Xenie Carroll turned away from the altar Mrs. John St. John, mistress of the handsomest house in the city and the most princely private fortune.

There was a flash of triumph in her dark eyes as she received the congratulations of her friends, yet her cheeks and lips were cold and white as marble.

But the light and color came back to her beautiful face when, in the same carriage that had taken her from her aunt's roof a poor, dependent girl, she was whirled back to the millionaire's splendid home to take her place as its queen.

The aged bridegroom scarcely felt equal to an extended bridal tour, so he had wisely eschewed a trip, and determined to inaugurate the reign of the new social star by a brilliant reception at his splendid residence.

All the beauties of art and nature were called in to further his design.

The elegant drawing-rooms were almost transformed into bowers of tropical bloom.

Beautiful birds fluttered their tropical plumage and caroled their sweet songs in the gilded cages that swung in the flowery arches and niches.

Music filled the air with entrancing strains, wooing light feet to the giddy dance.

In the spacious supper-room the tables shone with silver and gold and crystal, and every delicacy that could tempt the appetite from home or foreign shores was daintily served for the wedding-guests, with wines of the purest vintage and greatest age.

There was no lack of wealth, there was no lack of beauty in the brilliant assemblage that graced the millionaire's proud house that night; and she, his bride, was now the wealthiest, as she had ever been the loveliest, of them all, yet she stole away at length from her aged bridegroom's flatteries, and sought the solitude of the conservatory.

CHAPTER II.

The beautiful fragrance-breathing bower was deserted. The soft light of the wax-lights, half-hidden in flowers, streamed down upon her as she trod the leafy walks alone in her beautiful white satin robe, frosted with delicate lace, and her shining jewels that encircled a throat as white and round and queenly as if she had been a princess royal.

Yet none were here to praise the soft light of her dark eyes, the dazzling beauty of her smiles, the tender, tinted oval of her face.

Why was she here alone to "waste her sweetness on the desert air?"

Ah! in a moment she spoke in a stifled voice, her white hands twisted in the band of jewels that encircled her throat as if the beautiful flashing things burned her by their mere contact.

"I had to come here for a free breath away from that old man whose very presence stifles and smothers me. And yet—and yet, I am his wife! Oh, Heaven, what a terrible price I must pay for my revenge!"

She paused, and a strange look came into her eyes. It was a look of terrible dread and despair, inexplicably blended with passionate triumph.

"And yet," she began again, after a moment's silence, looking around at the evidences of wealth and taste so lavishly scattered about her, "what a glorious revenge it is! It was for this he scorned and deserted me! Yet I have stripped him of his heritage. I have stolen from him the empire he held so long. I have revenged myself tenfold for what I suffered at his hands. Ah! weak fool that I am, why regret the price of such a splendid triumph?"

Her face grew hard and cold, a cruel smile curled her scarlet lips, her eyes flashed with scorn.

Pride and passion spoke in every curve of her mobile, spirited face.

The lace hangings at the entrance parted noiselessly, and a man stepped lightly across the threshold.

Not a sound announced his presence, yet she looked up instantly, as if by some subtle inner sense she divined that he was there.

"Ah!" she breathed, in a hissing tone of hate and scorn.

A mocking smile curled the man's lip as he bowed before her.

"Ah! *ma tante*," he said, in a cool tone of scorn, "permit me to offer my congratulations."

Some emotion too great for utterance seemed to overpower her, so that she struggled vainly for speech a moment, while he stood silent, with folded arms, looking down at her from his haughty height with a look of veiled hatred in his dark-blue eyes.

They were deadly foes, this man and woman, yet nature had formed them as if for the perfect complement of each other.

He was tall, strong and fair, with the proud beauty and commanding air we fancy in the Grecian gods of old.

She was *petite*, dark, brilliant as a rose, and passionate as the tropical blood of the south could make her.

Breaking down the bars of her great emotion at last, she laughed aloud—a cool, insolent, incredulous laugh that made the hot blood bound faster through his veins, and a flush creep over his face.

"You call me aunt," she said; "ha! ha!"

"Yes, madam, you bear that relationship to me since your marriage with my uncle," he answered, with a formal bow.

"You expect to find me a most loving relative, no doubt?" she said, with exasperating coolness.

"I hope to do so, at least," he said, with calm frankness, "I cannot afford to quarrel with my uncle. I shall hope to keep on good terms with his wife."

"Ah! you don't wish to quarrel with your bread and butter," she said in a tone of cool contempt. "Well, *mon ami*, what do you suppose I married your uncle for?"

"The world says that you married him for his money," said the handsome young man, coolly.

"Yes, that is what the world says," she answered, with flashing eyes, and cresting her graceful head as haughtily as a young stag. "But you, Howard Templeton, you know better than that."

"Pardon me, how should I know better?" he rejoined, watching her keenly, as if it gave him a certain pleasure to irritate her. "The money seems to me the only reasonable excuse you had for taking him. My uncle, kindly be it spoken, for he has been my kindest friend, is neither young nor handsome. I credited you with better taste than to love such a homely old man!"

"You are right," she said, writhing under the keen sting of his words; "I did not marry him for love! Neither did I marry him for his money. I have never craved wealth for its own sake, though I have always known that a costly setting would befit beauty such as mine. I sold myself to that old man in yonder for revenge!"

"Revenge?" he repeated, inquiringly.

"Yes, upon *you*!" she repeated, with bitter frankness; "you sacrificed me that you might inherit your uncle's wealth. Love, hope, gladness, were stricken from my life at one fell blow. There was nothing left me but revenge upon my base deceiver. So I sold myself for the heritage you prized so highly that you might be left penniless."

"Yet once you loved me!" he muttered, half to himself.

"Yes, once I loved you," she answered, looking at him in proud scorn. "When my aunt brought me to the city two years ago a simple, unsophisticated country girl, you saw me and set yourself to win me by every art of which you were master. She encouraged you in your designs, for she knew that you were the reputed heir of your uncle, John St. John, and she thought it would be a fine match for the pretty little country girl. In the spring I went home with your ring upon my finger, the proudest girl in the world, and told mamma that you had promised to marry me. Then you came down to my country home and found out that the rich Mrs. Egerton's pretty niece was as poor as a church mouse. So you went back and told John St. John that you wanted to marry a girl who was beautiful but poor, and he—the old dotard, who had forgotten his youth, and transmuted his heart into gold—he bade you give me up on pain of disinheritance."

"And I obeyed him," said Howard Templeton, as she paused for breath.

"Yes, you obeyed him," she repeated; "you broke your plighted faith and word, you ruined my life, you broke my heart, you sold your truth and your honor to that cruel old man for his sordid gold, and now, to-night, you stand stripped of everything—and all because you turned a woman's love to hate."

She paused breathlessly and stood looking at him with blazing eyes and crimson cheeks, and lips parted in a smile of bitter triumph.

She had never looked more beautiful, yet it was a dangerous beauty, scathing to the man who looked upon her and knew that his sin had roused the terrible passions of revenge and hatred in her young heart.

"But Xenie, think a moment," he said. "I had been brought up by Uncle John as his heir. I did not know how to work. I never earned a cent in my whole life! When he swore he would disinherit me if I married you, what could I do? I had to give you up. You must have starved if I had married you against his will!"

"I would have starved with you, I loved you so!" she exclaimed passionately.

"Would you, really?" he asked, with a slight air of wonder; "well, they say that women love like that. For myself, I have never reached a stage as idiotic, though I own that I loved you to the verge of distraction, Xenie."

"Well, and what will you do now?" she asked, sneeringly. "You will have to starve at last without the pleasure of my company, for my husband shall never leave you one dollar of his money; I will poison his mind against you, I will make him hate you even as I hate you! I have sworn to have the bitterest revenge for my wrongs, and I will surely keep my vow!"

"I defy you," he answered, looking down at her from his superb height, his proud Saxon beauty ablaze with wrath and scorn. "I defy you to rob me of my uncle's heart or even of his fortune. He shall know what a traitress he has taken to his heart. I will dispute your empire with you and you shall find me a foeman worthy of your steel. You will find that it is a terrible thing to make a man who has loved you hate and defy you!"

"'The sweetest thing upon this earth is love.And next to love, the sweetest thing is hate.'"

She quoted with a wild, defiant laugh. "Well, Howard Templeton, I take up the gage of defiance that you have thrown down. We will wage the deadliest feud the world ever knew between man and woman! From this moment it shall be war to the knife!"

"So be it," he answered with a scowl of hatred as he turned upon his heel and passed through the lace hangings to mingle with the gay and thoughtless throng outside, while curious glances followed him on every side, for all knew that the foolish old bridegroom had promised to make Howard Templeton his heir.

CHAPTER III.

The beautiful bride remained motionless where Howard Templeton had left her until the rich lace curtains parted noiselessly again and her lawful lord and master looked in upon her.

He did not speak for a moment, so beautiful she looked standing still and pale as a statue beneath a tall rose-tree that showered its scented petals down upon her night-black hair with its crown of orange blossoms.

No subtle instinct warned her of his presence as it had when that other came.

She stood silent and pale, the dark lashes shading her rounded cheek, her white hands loosely clasped before her until he spoke:

"Xenie, my darling!"

She started and shivered as she looked up.

Mr. St. John came slowly to her side and drew her hand through his arm.

"My dear, I have been seeking you everywhere. Supper is announced," he said.

"I only came here just a little while ago for a quiet minute to myself," she said, apologetically.

"Ah! then, you like quiet and repose sometimes," he said; "I am glad of that, for I am not fond of gayety myself, at least not too much of it. I suppose I am getting too far into the sere and yellow leaf to enjoy it, eh, my dear?"

"I hope not; sir," she said, making an effort to throw off her preoccupation and enter into the conversation with interest.

After the splendid banquet had been served, he led her to a quiet seat and begged her not to dance again that evening.

"I am too old to dance myself," he said, "but I am so selfish I want to keep you by my side that I may feast my eyes upon your peerless beauty. Can you be contented with my society, love?" he inquired, giving her a curious look.

"I will do whatever pleases you best, sir," she said, with an inward shudder of disgust.

"Very well; we will sit here hand in hand like a veritable Darby and Joan, and enjoy each other's company," he said, giving her an affectionate smile.

The bride looked at her lord in surprise. She had not known him long, for their marriage had followed upon a brief acquaintance and hurried courtship.

Xenie had never thought him very brilliant, and, indeed, she had heard people say maliciously that the old man was getting weak-minded, but after all, the proposition to hold her hand before all that brilliant array of wedding-guests nearly staggered her.

She made some plausible excuse for keeping her hands in her own possession, and sat quietly by his side, watching the black coats of the men and the bright robes of the women as they fluttered through the joyous mazes of the dance.

"Do you see the lovely girl dancing with my nephew, Howard Templeton?" he said, to her after a short silence.

She looked up and saw Edith Wayland, one of her bridesmaids, whirling through the waltz in the arms of her deadly foe.

"Yes," she said, with a kind of stifled gasp.

"She's in love with my nephew," said the old man, with a low chuckle of pleasure.

"Indeed? Did she tell you so?" asked Mrs. St. John, half scornfully.

"Never mind how I found out. It's true, anyhow. And she is a great heiress, my dear, almost as rich as I am. I mean to make a match between her and my nephew."

"Do you?" she asked, but her voice was very low and faint, and the room swam around her so that the dancers seemed mingled in inextricable mazes.

"Yes, I do; but what is the matter with you, my darling?" he said, looking anxiously at her. "You have grown so pale!"

"It is nothing—a headache from the heat of the rooms," she murmured, confusedly, "but go on. You were saying——"

"That I am going to marry my nephew to Miss Wayland—yes. She is very rich, and he, well, the poor fellow, you know, Xenie, always expected to be my heir. And now, since my marriage, of course his prospects are entirely altered. He cannot expect much from me now. But I'm going to set him up with a few thousands, and marry him to the heiress. That's almost as well as leaving him my money—isn't it?" he laughed. "I've spoken to Howard about it, and he is pleased with the idea. There will be no difficulty with her, I am sure. Howard was always a lucky dog among the girls."

He laughed, and rubbed his withered palms softly together, and Xenie sat perfectly silent, her brain in a whirl, her pulse beating at fever heat.

Was this old man, whom she hated because his despotic will had blasted her brief dream of happiness, to despoil her of her revenge for which she had dared and risked so much?

And Howard Templeton—was her oath of vengeance of no avail, that fortune should make him her spoiled darling still?

The waltz music ceased with a great, passionate crash of melody, and the gentlemen led their partners to their seats.

Mr. St. John resigned his seat to Edith Wayland, and moved away on the arm of his nephew.

"What a handsome man Mr. Templeton is," said the lovely girl shyly to Mrs. St. John.

The bride looked after his retreating figure with a curl of her scarlet lip.

"Yes, he is as handsome as a Greek god," she said, "but then, he is utterly heartless—a mere fortune-hunter."

"Oh! Mrs. St. John, surely not," said Miss Wayland, in an anxious tone. "Why should you think so?"

"Perhaps it would suit you as well not to hear," said Mrs. St. John, with an arch insinuation in her look and tone.

"By no means. Pray tell me your reasons for what you said, Mrs. St. John," said the sweet, blue-eyed girl, blushing very much, and nervously fluttering her white satin fan.

"Well, since you are not particularly interested in him, I will tell you," was the careless reply. "I was engaged to Mr. Templeton myself, two winters ago—when I first came out, you know, dear! I suppose he thought I was wealthy, for Aunt Egerton dressed me elegantly, and lent me her diamonds. The summer after our engagement he came to the country to see me, and then he found out my poverty—for I will tell you candidly, Edith, my people are as poor as church mice—and, would you believe it? he went back and wrote me a letter, and told me he could not afford to marry for love—he must have an heiress or none. So our little affair was all over with then, you know."

She paused and looked away, for she knew that she had stabbed the girl's heart deeply, and she did not wish to witness the pain she had inflicted.

In a moment, however, Miss Wayland exclaimed, indignantly:

"Oh! Mrs. St. John, is it possible that Mr. Templeton could have treated you so cruelly and heartlessly?"

"It is quite true, Miss Wayland. If you doubt my word I give you *carte blanche* to ask my aunt, Mrs. Egerton, or even Mr. Templeton himself. You see I have the best reason in the world for accusing him of being a fortune-hunter."

The beautiful young girl did not think of doubting Mrs. St. John's assertion, although it caused her the bitterest pain.

There was an earnestness in the words and tones of the bride that carried conviction with them.

Miss Wayland sat musing quietly a moment, then she said, hesitatingly:

"May I ask if you are friends with Mr. Templeton now, Mrs. St. John?"

Xenie lifted her dark eyes and looked at the gentle girl.

"Should you love a man that won your heart and threw it away like a broken toy?" she asked, slowly.

"I do not believe that I could ever forgive him," said Edith, frankly.

"Nor can I," answered Xenie, in a low voice of repressed passion. "No, I am not friends with him, Edith, and never shall be; I am not the kind of woman who could forgive such a cruel slight."

Neither of them said another word on the subject, but Edith knew quite well from that moment why Xenie had married Mr. St. John.

"It was not for the sake of the money, but simply to revenge herself on Howard Templeton," she said to herself, with a woman's ready wit.

And when Mr. Templeton, according to his uncle's desire, offered her his hand and heart, a few days later, expecting to have her for the asking, he was surprised to receive a cold, almost contemptuous refusal.

But she dropped a few words before they parted by which he knew plainly that his deadly foe had been working against him, and that her revengeful hand had struck a fortune from his grasp for the second time in the space of a week.

CHAPTER IV.

Several months of irksome quiet to Mrs. St. John succeeded the festivities that followed upon her marriage.

Her elderly bridegroom found that protracted gayeties did not agree with his age and health, and with the obstinacy common to a selfish old age, he prohibited his wife from participation in those scenes of pleasure in which, by reason of her youth and beauty, she was so pre-eminently fitted to shine.

He could not stand such excitement himself, he said, and he wanted his wife at home to cheer and solace his declining years.

So the beautiful bridal dresses hung in the wardrobe unworn, and the costly jewels hid their brightness locked away in their caskets.

Xenie had small need for these things in the lonely life to which she found herself condemned by her foolish, doting old husband.

Loving pleasure and excitement with all the ardor of a passionate, impulsive temperament like hers, it is quite possible that Mrs. St. John might have rebelled against her liege lord's selfishness, but for one strong purpose to which she bent every energy, subordinating everything else to its accomplishment.

So she bore his selfish exactions with a patient, yielding sweetness, and ministered to his caprices with the beautiful devotion of a fireside angel.

She was using every sweet persuasion in her power to induce Mr. St. John to execute a will in her favor.

She had learned that in the event of his death, without a will, his widow would legally inherit only one-third of his great wealth, while the remaining two-thirds would descend to his next of kin—the next of kin in this case being her enemy, Howard Templeton.

Xenie knew that her revenge would not be secure until her husband had made his will and cut off his nephew without a dollar.

She had believed that Mr. St. John's infatuation for her would make her task easy, but she had not counted upon the uneasy sense in the old man's mind of a certain injustice done to the nephew he had reared, by his unexpected marriage.

"No, no, Xenie," he said, when she openly pleaded with him to make such a will. "It would be unjust to leave poor Howard without a dollar to support himself."

"He is a man," said Xenie, scornfully. "He has his head and hands to earn his living."

"Yes; but Howard does not know how to work, my darling, and it is all my fault. I brought him up as my heir and refused to let him have a profession or to learn anything useful. You see we are the last of our race, and I expected to leave him everything when I died. I did not know I should meet and marry you, my darling," he said, kissing her fondly, without noticing her uncontrollable shiver of disgust.

"Yes, but your marriage alters everything," she said, eagerly, lifting her melting, dark eyes to his face with a siren smile on the curve of her scarlet lips. "You would not wish to leave your money away from me, your poor, helpless little wife?"

"There is enough for you both, my dear," he said, persuasively. "Howard might have his share—the smaller share, of course—and you would still be a wealthy woman!"

"I hate Howard Templeton!" exclaimed Xenie, with sudden, passionate vehemence.

The old man looked at her half angrily.

"You hate my nephew?" he said. "Why do you hate him, Xenie, when next to you I love him, best of anyone in the world?"

Xenie's sober senses, that had almost deserted her in her sudden gust of passion, returned to her with a gasp.

"I—oh, forgive me," she said, with ready penitence, "I spoke foolishly. I do not like you to love him so. I am jealous of you, my darling!"

She leaned toward him and laid her white arm around his shoulder caressingly.

But suddenly, and even as she lifted her beautiful face for his caress, he drew back his hand, and without a word of warning, struck her a heavy blow across the face.

She reeled backward and fell upon the floor, the red blood spurting from her nostrils and from her lips that the terrible blow had driven against the points of her white teeth and terribly lacerated.

"You Jezebel," he shouted, hoarsely, rising and standing over her with his brandished fist. "How dare you hate him—my own nephew, my handsome Howard!"

With a moan of fear and pain Xenie sprang up and fled to the furthest corner of the room.

"Oh! you coward!" she cried, passionately. "To strike a woman—a helpless woman!"

She was trying to staunch the fast flowing blood with her lace handkerchief, but she stopped and stared at him in dumb terror as he approached her.

For the glare of madness shone in his dim eyes as they turned upon her—his foam-flecked lips were drawn away from his glistening set of false teeth, and his face presented a terrible appearance.

"Oh! my God, he is going to kill me!" she moaned to herself, crouching down in the corner with her arms raised wildly above her shrinking head.

He towered above her with his clenched fist raised threateningly and his eyes glaring ferociously upon her.

Xenie believed that a sudden frenzy of madness had come upon her husband and that he was going to take her life.

She was about to shriek aloud in the hope of rescue, when he suddenly clapped a strong hand over her lips.

"Hush!" he said, fearfully, "hush, Xenie, don't let anyone know I struck you! Does it hurt you much?—the blood, I mean—I'm sorry if it does."

The tone was that of a wheedling, penitent child that is sorry for its fault. In sheer surprise the frightened creature looked up at him.

The ferocious look of bloodthirsty madness had marvelously faded from his face, and left a pale, fearful, childish expression instead.

He dropped his hand and wiped the blood from it, shivering all over.

"Oh! the blood, how red it is!" he whined. "Did I hurt you, my love? I'm sorry—very sorry. Don't tell anyone I struck you."

"I'll tell the whole world," she flashed forth, speaking with difficulty, for her lips were bruised and swollen. "I'll tell them that you are mad, and I'll have you put into an asylum for dangerous lunatics, you base coward!"

Mr. St. John's face grew livid at her angry threat. He trembled with fear.

"No, no, Xenie, you won't, you mustn't do it," he gasped forth. "I will never do so again. I'll be your slave if you won't tell!"

"I will tell it everywhere!" cried his young wife, rushing to the door, her whole passionate spirit aglow with the keenest resentment.

But with unlooked-for strength in one of his age, he ran forward, and stood with his back against the door.

"You shall not go till you promise to keep silent," he said, firmly; "I will do anything you ask me, Xenie, if you will only not tell on me!"

"Anything?" she exclaimed, turning quickly.

"Yes, anything," he reiterated, with a weak, imploring look, full of craven fear.

"Very well," she answered firmly; "make your will to-day, and cut Howard Templeton off with a shilling, and I'll keep your secret—otherwise the city shall ring with the story of your cruelty!"

"Won't you let me leave him ten thousand dollars, dear?" he asked, pitifully.

"Not a dollar!" she answered coldly.

"Five thousand dollars?"

"Not a dollar!" she reiterated firmly.

"Very well," he answered, weakly. "I have said you shall name your own price. Shall I go to my lawyer now, Xenie?"

"Yes, now," she answered, with a flash of triumph in her eyes.

He stood still a moment looking at her with a half-insane look of cunning on the wrinkled features that but a moment ago had been transformed by maniacal rage.

"Poor boy!" he said, "you hate him very much, Xenie; I wonder what he has done to make you his enemy!"

She did not answer, and the old millionaire went out of the room, after turning upon her a strange look of blended cunning and triumph which she could not understand.

"Pshaw! he meant nothing by it," she said to herself to dispel the uneasy impression that glance had left. "The old man is getting weak and silly. One is scarcely safe alone with him."

She shuddered at the recollection of what she had passed through, and going to her private room, locked the door and bathed her swollen, discolored face with a healing lotion.

CHAPTER V.

Xenie remained alone in her chamber until darkness gathered like a pall over every luxurious object about her. Her maid came and tapped at the door once, but she sent her away, saying that her head ached and she did not wish to be disturbed.

It was quite true, for her heavy fall upon the floor had hurt her severely; so she remained quietly lying on a sofa until black darkness hid everything from her confused sight.

Then there came a light tap upon the door again. She thought it was the maid to light the gas.

"You may go away, Finette, I do not need you yet," she said, feeling that the darkness suited her mood the best.

"It is I, Xenie. Open the door. I wish to speak to you," said her husband's voice.

She went to the door, unlocked and threw it wide open. The light from the hall streamed in upon her pale and haggard face, her dress in disorder, her dark hair loose and dishevelled.

"It is dark in there, I cannot see you, my darling," he said; "come across into my smoking-room in the light. I want to tell you something."

He took her hand and drew her across the hall into a luxurious apartment he called his smoking-room.

It was elegantly furnished with cushioned easy-chairs and lounges, while the floor was covered with a soft, Persian carpet and beautiful rugs.

The marble mantel was decorated with costly meerschaums, and chibouques of various patterns and materials, and a richly gilded box stood in the center, containing cigars and perfumed smoking tobacco.

On a marble-topped table in the center of the room stood two bottles of wine, and two richly-chased drinking glasses.

"Well?" she inquired, half-fearfully, as he drew her in and carefully closed the door.

"I have made my will, dear," he said, looking at her with a curious smile.

"And you have cut Howard Templeton off without a shilling?" she said, anxiously.

"Yes, darling, I have made you the sole heir to all my wealth," answered the old man, drawing his arm around her shrinking form. "But perhaps you will wish the old man dead, now, that you may enjoy his money without any incumbrance."

"Oh! no," she exclaimed quickly, for something in his words touched her heart, and made her forget for a moment that cruel blow from his hand. "Oh! no, I shall never wish you dead, and I thank you a thousand times for your generosity."

"Then you forgive me for my—for that—to-day?" he inquired in a flighty, half-frightened way, fixing his dim eyes on her beautiful face with an anxious expression.

"Yes, I forgive you freely," she said, touched again, as she scarcely thought she could be, by his looks and tones, and yet longing to get away, for she was half-frightened by a certain inexplicable wildness about him. "And now I must go and dress for dinner."

"Wait, I have not done with you yet," he said, catching her tightly around the wrist, his restlessness increasing. "I saw my nephew on the street, and brought him home with me to dinner. Do you care, Xenie?"

"No, I do not care," she answered, steadily, yet her heart gave a great passionate throb of bitter anger.

Still holding her tightly by the hand he pulled open the door and sent his voice ringing loudly down the hall.

"Howard, Howard, come here!"

Xenie heard the distant door of the library unclose, then shut again, and a man's footsteps ringing along the marble hall.

She tried to wrench her hand away and flee, but it was useless. He held her as in a vise.

"Let me go," she panted, "my hair is down, my dress is disarranged, my face is disfigured, I do not wish to meet him."

But he held her tightly, gnashing his teeth in sudden rage at her efforts to escape.

At that moment Howard Templeton entered the room.

He started back as his gaze encountered Mrs. St. John's, then with a cold bow stood still, turning an inquiring glance upon his uncle's excited face.

"I want you to take a glass of wine with me, Howard," said his uncle in a cordial tone. "Xenie, my love, you will pour the wine for us."

He led her forward, to the little marble-topped table where stood the wine and glasses.

She saw that the corks were both drawn from the bottles, and taking up one she poured some of its contents into the richly-chased glass beside it.

"Now pour from the second bottle into the second glass," commanded her husband.

Xenie silently obeyed him, without a thought as to the strangeness of the request, for her heart was beating almost to suffocation with the bitter consciousness of her enemy's presence.

Mr. St. John watched her every motion with a strange, repressed excitement.

His eyes glittered, his lips worked as if he were talking to himself. He nodded to his nephew as she stepped back.

"Let us drink long life and happiness to Mrs. St. John," he said.

Howard Templeton took one glass, and his uncle took the remaining one.

Both bowed to the shrinking woman who stood watching them, drained their glasses, and set them back with a simultaneous clink upon the marble table.

Then a wild, maniacal laugh filled the room—so shrill, so exultant, so blood-curdling, it froze the blood in the veins of the man and woman who stood there listening.

"Ha, ha," cried Mr. St. John, "you thought I did not know your secret, you two! But I did. I heard your talk on my wedding-night. I knew then that I had taken the woman you loved. Howard, I knew that she had sought me, and won me, and married me, to revenge her wrongs at your hands. I said to myself her beautiful body is mine—I have bought it with my gold—but her heart is Howard Templeton's!"

"No, no," cried Xenie, stamping her foot passionately; "I hate him! I hate him!"

"Hush!" thundered the old man, turning on her with the wild glare of madness in his eyes, "hush, woman! I have thought it over for months—at last I have reached a conclusion. The world is not wide enough for us two men to live in. So I said to myself—one of us must die!"

"Must die!" repeated Howard Templeton, with a sudden strong shudder.

"Yes, *die*!" cried the maniac, with another horrible laugh. "So I put deadly poison into one of the bottles that chance might decide our fates. Xenie poured out death for one of us just now. In ten minutes either you or I will be dead, Howard Templeton!"

CHAPTER VI.

For one terrible moment Xenie St. John and Howard Templeton remained silently gazing at the excited old man, as if petrified with horror, then:

"My God, my uncle is a madman!" broke hoarsely from the young man's ashen lips, in tones of unutterable horror and grief.

Mrs. St. John rushed to the door, threw it wide open, and shrieked aloud in frenzied accents for help.

The servants came rushing in and found their old master crouching in a corner of the room, gibbering and mouthing like some terrible wild beast, his bloodshot eyes rolling in their sockets, his lips all flecked with foam, while Howard Templeton remained silent in the center of the room, like a statue of horror.

"A doctor—bring a doctor!" shrieked Xenie, wildly.

It was not five minutes before a physician, living close by, was brought in, but even as he crossed the threshold, the insane creature rolled over upon the floor in the agonies of death.

One or two desperate struggles, a gasp, a quiver from head to foot and the old millionaire lay dead before them.

The physician knelt down and felt his heart and his pulse.

"He is dead," he said, shaking his head slowly and sadly. "I apprehended a fit the last time he consulted me, some three weeks ago. His mind and body were both weakening fast. This mournful end was not unexpected by me."

Mrs. St. John made a quick step forward.

She was about to say, "He did not die in a fit, doctor, he died of poison," when a hand like steel gripped her wrist.

She looked up and met the stern, awful gaze of Howard Templeton.

"Hush!" he whispered, hurriedly and sternly. "Let the world accept the physician's verdict. Say nothing of what you know. Do not brand his memory with the terrible obloquy of insanity and self-murder!"

As he spoke he turned away, and crossed the room, and as he passed the marble-topped table, it fell over, no one could have told how, and the bottles and glasses were shivered upon the floor.

One of the servants removed the *debris*, and mopped up the spilled wine from the floor, and no one thought anything more of it.

Yet, by that simple act, Howard Templeton saved his uncle's name and his own from the shafts of malice and calumny that must have assailed them if the terrible truth had come to light.

So the physician's hasty verdict of apoplexy was universally accepted by the world, and the old millionaire was laid away in his costly tomb a few days later, regretted by all his friends, and the secret of his tragic death was locked in the breasts of two who kept that hideous story sacred, although they were deadly foes.

Yes, deadly foes, and destined to hate each other more and more, for when the old millionaire's papers were examined, the beautiful widow found that she was foiled of her dearly-bought revenge at last.

For no will was found, although Xenie protested passionately that her husband had made a will the very last day of his life.

The most careful and assiduous search failed to reveal the existence of any legal document like a will, and the lawyers gravely assured Mrs. St. John that she could claim only a third of her deceased husband's wealth, the remainder falling to the next of kin, Howard Templeton.

"You see, madam," said the old lawyer, whom she was anxiously questioning, "if Mr. St. John had left a child, you could claim the whole estate as its lawful guardian, even without the existence of a will. But there being no nearer kin than Mr. Templeton, it legally falls to him, after you receive your widow's portion."

The young widow brooded over those words night and day.

She hated Howard Templeton more than ever.

She would have given the whole world, had it been hers, to wrest that fortune from her enemy's grasp, and leave him poor and friendless to fight his way through the hard world.

"Oh! if I only could find that will," she thought wildly. "Is it true that Mr. St. John made it, or was he deceiving me? He was utterly insane. Could one expect truth from a madman?"

Gradually, as weary weeks flew by, she began to believe that Mr. St. John had deceived her.

She felt quite sure in her own mind, after a little while, that he had never made the will.

He had fully meant for Howard Templeton to inherit his wealth.

Yet bitterly as she regretted its loss she could not bring herself to hate the memory of the old man she had married, and who had loved her for a little while with so fond and foolish a passion.

The memory of his dreadful death was too strong upon her.

She woke at night from dreadful dreams that recalled that last awful day of her husband's life, and lay shuddering and weeping, and praying to forget that fearful face, and blood-curdling, maniacal laugh that still rung in her shocked hearing.

"You are growing thin and pale, Xenie," Mrs. Egerton said, when she came to condole with her, more for the loss of the fortune than the loss of her husband. "People are talking of your ill looks, and they say you take Mr. St. John's death so hard, you must have cared for him more than anyone believed. I let them talk, for, of course, it is very much to your credit to have them think so, but as I know better myself, I cannot help wondering at your paleness and trouble."

"It was all so sudden and terrible," murmured the young widow, as she lay back in her easy-chair, looking very fragile and beautiful in her deep mourning dress.

"Yes it was very bad his going off in a fit that way," said her aunt. "Still, it was to be expected, Xenie. He was very old, and really growing childish, I thought. His going off without a will was the worst part of it. Of course it hurt you terribly for Templeton to have the money!"

The sudden flash in Mrs. St. John's dark eyes told plainer than words how much it had hurt her.

"However, Xenie, I would give over worrying about it," continued her aunt, soothingly.

"But my revenge, Aunt Egerton. Think how much I sacrificed for it. I married that foolish old man, and endured his caprices so long without a murmur, allowed myself to be shut up in solitude like a bird in a cage, and never murmured at his tiresome exactions. And all for what? Because I expected to get his whole fortune, and be revenged on the coward who broke my heart for the sake of it. And to be despoiled of my revenge like this is too hard for endurance," she exclaimed, walking up and down the room, and wringing her white hands in a perfect passion of despair and regret.

"Oh! let the wretch go," said Mrs. Egerton, complacently rustling in her silks and laces. "You have secured a large portion of the estate, anyhow. And you are so young and beautiful still, Xenie, you may even marry a greater fortune than that, when your year of mourning is expired."

Xenie stopped still in her excited walk, and looked at her aunt.

"I shall never marry again—never," she said earnestly. "I have as much money as I want, only—only I want to take that from Howard Templeton because I want to humble him and wring his heart. And there is but one way to do it, and that is to reduce him to poverty. Money is the only god he worships!" she added bitterly.

"He treated you villainously and deserves to be punished," said Mrs. Egerton, "but still I would try to forget it, Xenie. You will lose your youth and prettiness brooding over this idea of revenge."

"I will never forget it," cried Mrs. St. John, wrathfully. "I will wait and watch, and if ever I see a chance to punish Howard Templeton, I shall strike swiftly and surely."

Her aunt arose, gathering her silken wrappings about her tall, elegant form.

"Well, I must go now," she said. "I see it is of no use talking to you. Come and see me when you feel better, Xenie."

"I am going to the country next week," said her niece, abruptly.

"Indeed? Has not your mother been up to see you in your trouble?" inquired Mrs. Egerton, pausing in her graceful exit.

"No. I wrote to her, but she has neither come nor written. I fear something has happened. She is usually very punctual. Anyway, I shall go down next week and stay with them a week or two."

"I hope the change may improve your spirits, love," said her aunt, kissing her and going out with an airy "*Au revoir.*"

CHAPTER VII.

"Mamma, how pale and troubled you look. What ails you?"

Mrs. St. John was crossing the threshold of the little cottage home that looked, oh, so poor and cheap after the stately brown-stone palace she had left that morning, and after one quick glance into her mother's careworn face she saw that new lines of grief and trouble had come upon it since last they had met.

"Come up into my room, Xenie. I have much to say to you," said her mother, leading the way up the narrow stairway into her bedroom, a neat and scrupulously clean little room, but plainly and almost poorly furnished.

Mrs. Carroll was a widow with only a few barren acres of land, which she hired a man to till. Her husband was long since dead, and the burden of rearing her two children had been a heavy one to the lonely widow, who came of a good family and naturally desired to do well by her two daughters, both of them being gifted with uncommon beauty.

But poverty had hampered and crushed her desires, and made her an old woman while yet she was in the prime of life.

Xenie removed her traveling wraps and sat down before the little toilet glass to arrange her disordered hair.

"My dear, how pale and sad you look in your widow's weeds," said Mrs. Carroll, regarding her attentively. "I was very sorry to hear of your husband's death. It is very sad to be left a widow so young—barely twenty."

"Yes," answered Xenie, abstractedly; then she turned around and said abruptly: "Mamma, where is my sister?"

Mrs. Carroll looked at her daughter a moment without replying.

"I have brought her some beautiful presents," continued Mrs. St. John, "and you, too, dear mamma—things that you will like—both beautiful and useful."

Mrs. Carroll looked at her daughter a moment in utter silence, and her lips quivered strangely.

Then she caught up a corner of her homely check apron, and hiding her convulsed face in its folds, she burst into bitter weeping.

Xenie sprang up and threw her arms around the neck of the agitated woman.

"Oh, mamma," she cried, anxiously, "speak to me. Tell me what ails you? Where is Lora?"

As if that name had power to open the flood gates of emotion wider, Mrs. Carroll wept more bitterly than ever.

"Mamma, you frighten me," cried Xenie, terrified. "Oh, tell me where is Lora? Is she dead?"

"No, no—oh, better that she were!" sobbed her mother, wildly.

Mrs. St. John grew as pale as death. She shook her mother almost rudely by the arm.

"What has Lora done?" she cried. "Where is she? I will go and seek her."

She was rushing wildly to the door, but Mrs. Carroll sprang forward, and catching the skirt of her dress, pulled her back.

"Not now!" she gasped; "wait a little. That wretched girl has ruined her good name and disgraced us all."

Mrs. St. John dropped into a chair like one bereft of life, and her great, black eyes, dilated with terror, stared up into her mother's face.

"Yes, it is too true," said her mother, sitting down and rocking herself back and forth, while low and heart-broken moans escaped her white lips.

"But, mamma, poor, good, little Lora! it cannot be! She was truth and innocence itself," panted the young widow, in a voice of anguish.

"She deceived us all—she was a sly little piece. You will see for yourself, Xenie. She lies ill in her chamber, and—and in a few months there will be a"—she lowered her voice and gave a fearful glance around her—"*a child*!"

"Oh! mamma, then she was married? Of course Lora was married! Doesn't she say so?" exclaimed Xenie, confidently.

"Oh, yes, she swears to a marriage—a secret one—but look you, Xenie—not a ring, not a witness, not a scrap of paper to prove it! And the man dead—lost at sea!" said Mrs. Carroll, despairingly.

"Oh! mamma, then it was——"

"Jack Mainwaring—yes. He was courting her this long time, you know. He asked for her, and I wouldn't give my consent. I thought he wasn't good enough for her—a sailor, and only second mate, you know. And Aunt Egerton had promised to give her a season in town this winter, and she might have made a better match than a sailor."

Mrs. Carroll broke down again and wept bitterly.

"Try to control yourself, mamma," said the young widow, stroking the bowed head tenderly. "And so Jack married her in spite of you?"

"Yes," sobbed her mother, "he married her secretly, she says. It was about the same time, or nearly, that you were married. He found out that Lora was going to town to be one of the bridesmaids, and was jealous, I suppose, thinking she might see someone she could like better. So he persuaded her into it, and they were to keep it secret until he came back from this voyage."

"And he is lost at sea, you say?" asked Xenie, thoughtfully.

"Yes; he went away in a few weeks after the marriage, to be gone six months; but the news came last week of the loss of his ship by fire, and his name was on the list of the dead. You see, Xenie, what a terrible position Lora was placed in. She fainted when she heard the news, and then I found out everything."

"Does anyone else know, mamma?" inquired Xenie, anxiously.

"Not yet. She has been ill, but I have cared for her myself, and did not call in the doctor. But we cannot keep it a secret always. Of course malicious people will not believe in the marriage, and Lora's fair fame will be ruined forever! Oh! if she had only never been born!" cried the proud and unhappy mother.

Mrs. St. John sat silent, her lily-white hands clasped in her lap, her dark eyes staring into vacancy with a strangely intent expression. She roused herself at last and looked at her mother.

"Mamma, we must devise ways and means of keeping this a secret! It would ruin the family to have it known," she said, decidedly.

"Yes, I know that," said Mrs. Carroll, gloomily. "I would do anything in the world to save Lora's fair fame if I only knew what to do!"

"I have a plan," said Xenie, rising quietly. "I will tell it you by-and-by, mamma. Everything shall come right if you will be guided by me. Now take me to my sister, if you please."

Mrs. Carroll rose silently and opened the door. Xenie followed her down a narrow passage to a door at the further end, and they entered a pretty and neat little room.

A low wood fire burned on the cleanly swept hearth, and on the white bed, with her dark hair trailing loosely over the pillows, lay a beautiful, white-faced girl, enough like Xenie to be her twin.

She started up with a cry of mingled joy and pain as the new-comer came toward her.

"My poor darling!" Mrs. St. John murmured, in a tone of infinite love and compassion, as she twined her arms around the trembling form.

Lora clung to her sister, sobbing and weeping convulsively. At length she whispered against her shoulder:

"Mamma has told you all, Xenie?"

"Yes, dear," was the gentle answer.

"And you—you believe that I was married?" questioned the invalid.

"Yes, darling," whispered her sister, tenderly. "How could I believe evil of you, my innocent, little Lora?"

"Thank God!" cried the invalid, gratefully. "Oh! Xenie, mamma has been so angry it nearly broke my heart."

"She will forgive you, darling," murmured Mrs. St. John, fondly, as she stroked the dark head nestling on her breast.

"And, oh, Xenie, poor Jack—my Jack—he is dead!" sobbed Lora, bursting into a fit of wild, hysterical weeping.

"There, darling, hush—you must not excite yourself," said Mrs. St. John, laying her sister back upon the pillows, and trying to soothe her frenzied excitement.

"And no one will believe that I was Jack's wife—I am disgraced forever! Mamma says so. The finger of scorn will be pointed at me everywhere. But what do I care, since my heart is broken? I only want to die!" moaned the unhappy young creature, as she tossed to and fro upon the bed.

"Be quiet, Lora; listen to me," said Mrs. St. John, taking the restless, white hands in her own, and sitting down upon the bed. "I wish to talk to you as soon as you become reasonable."

Thus adjured, Lora hushed her sobs by a great effort, and lay perfectly still but for the uncontrollable heaving of her troubled breast, her large, hollow, dark eyes fixed earnestly on Xenie's pale and lovely face.

Mrs. Carroll crouched down in a chair by the side of the bed, the image of hopeless woe.

"Lora, dear," said her sister, in low, earnest tones, "of course you know that, if this dreadful thing becomes known, the disgrace will be reflected upon us all."

Mrs. Carroll groaned, and Lora murmured a pitiful yes.

"I have thought of a plan to save you," continued Mrs. St. John. "A clever plan that would shield your fair fame forever. But it will require some co-operation on your part, and it may be that you and mamma may refuse for you to undertake it."

"You may count on my consent beforehand!" groaned Mrs. Carroll, desperately.

"I will do whatever mamma says," murmured Lora, weakly.

Mrs. St. John looked away from them a moment in silent thought; then she said, slowly:

"Of course, you know, mamma, that my husband died without a will, and that Howard Templeton inherited the greater part of his wealth?"

"Yes; you wrote me. I was very sorry that you were disappointed, dear," said her mother, gently, yet wondering what this had to do with Lora's forlorn case.

"Mamma," said Xenie, slowly, "if my husband had left me as Lora's left her, I could have kept that fortune out of Howard Templeton's hands."

"My dear, I hardly understand you," said her mother, blankly.

"Mamma, I mean that if I could hope for an heir to my husband, the child would inherit all that wealth, and Howard Templeton be left penniless."

"Oh, yes, I understand you now," was the quick reply, "but you have no prospect, no hope of such a thing—have you, dear?"

There was a moment's silence, and Mrs. St. John's fair face grew scarlet, then deadly white again. She looked away from her mother, and said, slowly:

"Yes, mamma, I have such a hope. Listen to me, you and Lora, and I will help you in your trouble, and you shall help me to complete my revenge."

CHAPTER VIII.

Some three or four weeks after Mrs. St. John's visit to the country, Howard Templeton was sitting in his club one day, smoking and reading, after a most luxurious lunch.

The young fellow looked very comfortable as he leaned back in his cushioned chair, the blue smoke curling in airy rings over his curly, blonde head, a look of lazy contentment in his handsome blue eyes.

He was somewhat of a Sybarite in his tastes, this handsome young fellow, over whose head twenty-five happy years had rolled serenely, without a shadow to mar their brightness save that unfortunate love affair two years before.

Howard was, emphatically, one of the "gilded youth" of his day. He "toiled not, neither did he spin." He had been cradled in luxury's silken lap all his life long.

Sorrow had passed him tenderly by as one exempt from the common ills of life.

He was so accustomed to his good luck that he seldom gave a thought to it. It simply seemed to him that he would go on that way forever.

Yet, to-day, for a wonder, he had been a little thoughtfully reviewing the events of the past six months.

"It was very kind in Uncle John to leave things so comfortable for me," he said to himself. "I thought his wife would influence him against me so much that he wouldn't have left me a penny. If he hadn't, what the deuce should I have done?"

He paused a moment, in comical amusement, to survey the situation; but the idea was too stupendous.

He could not even fancy himself the victim of adversity, much less tell what he would have done in that case. He laughed at it after a moment.

"I cannot even imagine it," he thought. "Poor little Xenie, how hard it went with her to be foiled in her revenge, as she called it. How she must have loved me to have turned against me so when I gave her up! Who would have believed that we two should ever hate each other with such a deadly hate?"

Something like a smothered sigh went upward with the blue cigar smoke, and just then a footstep crossed the threshold, and a man's voice said, lightly:

"Halloo, Doctor Templeton; enjoying yourself, as usual."

"Halloo, Doctor Shirley," returned Templeton, with a lazy nod at the new-comer. "Have a smoke?"

"I don't care if I do," said the doctor, throwing himself down in an easy-chair opposite the speaker, and lighting a weed. "How deuced comfortable you look, my boy!"

"Feel that way," lisped Templeton, in a lazy tone.

"Ah! I don't think you would feel so devil-may-care if you knew all that I know, old boy," laughed the doctor, significantly.

The old doctor was very well known at the club as a gossip, so Templeton only laughed carelessly as he said:

"What's the matter, doctor? Any of my sweethearts sick or dead?"

"Not that I know of," said Doctor Shirley. "However, Templeton, if any of your sweethearts has money, take my advice, young fellow, and make up to her without delay."

Howard Templeton laughed at the doctor's sage advice.

"Thanks," he said, "but I do very well as I am, doctor. I don't care to become a subject for petticoat government, yet."

"Yet things looked that way two years ago," said Doctor Shirley, maliciously, for Templeton's ardent devotion to Mrs. Egerton's lovely *debutante* at that time had been no secret in society.

Templeton's blonde face flushed a dark red all over, yet he laughed carelessly.

"Oh, yes, I had the fever," he said. "However, its severity then precludes the danger of ever having a second attack. How little I dreamed that she would be my aunt."

"Or your *bete noire*," said the doctor.

"Hardly that," said Templeton, composedly, as he knocked the ashes from the end of his cigar. "True, she has taken a slice of my fortune away, but then there's yet enough to butter my bread."

"There may not be much longer," said Doctor Shirley, meaningly.

"What do you mean?" asked Templeton, looking at him as if he had serious doubts of his sanity. "Who's going to take it away from me? Has Mrs. St. John found the will she talked of so much?"

"No," said Doctor Shirley, "but she has found something that will serve her as well."

"Confound it, doctor, I don't understand you at all," said the young fellow, a little testily. "What are you driving at, anyway?"

"Templeton, honestly, I hate to tell you," said the physician, sobering down, "but I've bad news for you. You know that Mrs. St. John has been ill lately, I suppose?"

"Yes, I heard it—thought, perhaps, she meant to shuffle off this mortal coil and leave me the balance of my uncle's property," said the young man, imperturbably.

"Nothing further from her thoughts, I assure you," was the laughing reply. "She has been quite ill, but she is well enough to come down into the drawing-room to-day. Come, now, Templeton, guess what I have to tell you?"

"'Pon honor, doctor, I haven't the faintest idea. Does it refer to my fair and respected aunt? Is it a new freak of hers?"

"Yes, decidedly a new freak," said the doctor, laughing heartily, and enjoying his joke very much.

"Well, then, out with it," said Howard, growing impatient. "Does she accuse me of stealing and secreting that fabulous missing will?"

"Not that I am aware of," and Doctor Shirley rose and threw away his half-smoked cigar, saying, carelessly: "I must be going. We poor devils of doctors never have time to smoke a whole cigar. Say, Templeton, Mrs. St. John has her mother and sister staying with her. Deuced handsome girl, that Lora Carroll! Very like her sister! And—don't go off in a fit, now, Templeton—in a very few months there will be a little heir to your deceased uncle's name and fortune!"

"I don't believe it!" exclaimed Howard Templeton, springing to his feet, while his handsome face grew white and red by turns.

"You don't believe it? That's because you don't want to believe it. But I give you my word and honor as a professional man and her medical attendant, that it is a self-evident fact," and laughing at his, little joke, the gossiping old doctor hurried away from the club-room.

CHAPTER IX.

"I don't believe it!" Howard Templeton repeated angrily, as he stood still where Doctor Shirley had left him, those unexpected words ringing through his brain.

"What is it you don't believe, Templeton?" inquired one of the "gilded youth," dawdling in and overhearing the remark.

"I don't believe anything—that's my creed," answered Templeton, snatching his hat, and hurrying out. He wanted to be out in the cold, fresh air. Somehow it seemed to him as if a hand grasped his throat, choking his life out.

He walked aimlessly up and down the crowded thoroughfare, seemingly blind and deaf to all that went on around him.

Men's eyes remarked the tall, well-proportioned form and handsome, blonde face with envy.

Women looked after him admiringly, thinking how splendid it would be to have such a man for a lover. Howard heeded nothing of it. He was accustomed to it. He simply took it for his due, and he had other things to engross his mind now.

"It can't be true, it can't be true," he said to himself, again and again in his restless walk. "It is the most undreamed of thing. Who could believe it?"

And yet it troubled him despite his incredulity. It troubled him so much that he went to see a lawyer about it.

He stated the case, and asked him frankly what were his chances if such a thing really should happen.

"No chance at all," was the grim reply. "If you did not resign your claim, Mrs. St. John would naturally sue you for the money on behalf of the legal heir."

"And then?" asked Howard.

"The case would certainly go against you."

Howard went out again and took another walk. He tried to fancy himself—Howard Templeton, the golden youth—face to face with the grim fiend, poverty.

He wondered how it would feel to earn his dinner before he ate it, to wear out his old coats, and have to count the cost of new ones, as he had vaguely heard that poor men had to do.

"I can't imagine it," he said to himself. "Time enough to bother my brain with such conundrums if the thing really comes to pass. And if it does, what a glorious triumph it will be for 'mine enemy!' I'd like to see her—by Jove, I believe I'll go there."

He stopped short, filled with the new idea, then hurried on, recalled to himself by a stare of surprise from a casual passer-by.

"Yes; why shouldn't I go there, by George?" he went on. "It was my home before she came there. The world doesn't know that we are 'at outs,' although we are sworn foes privately. I'll pretend to call on Lora Carroll. Lora was a pretty girl enough when I was down there that summer, young and unformed, though time has remedied that defect, doubtless. Doctor Shirley thought her handsome. Yes, I will call on little Lora. A daring thing to do, perhaps, but then I'm in the mood for daring a great deal."

The lamps were lighted and the glare of the gas flared down upon him as he thus made up his mind.

He went to his hotel, made an elaborate and elegant toilet, as if anxious to please, then sallied forth toward the brown-stone palace where his enemy reigned in triumph.

A soft and subdued light shone through the curtains of rose-colored silk and creamy lace that shaded the windows of the drawing-room. A fancy seized upon Howard to peep through them before he went up the marble steps and sent in his card.

"For who knows that they may decline to see me," he thought, "and I am determined to get one look at Xenie. I want to see if she looks very happy over her triumph."

He glanced around, saw that no one was passing, and cautiously went up to the window.

It was as much as he could do, tall as he was, to peer into the room by standing on tiptoe.

He looked into the beautiful and spacious room where he had spent many happy hours with his deceased uncle in years gone by, and a sigh to the memory of those old days breathed softly over his lips, and a dimness came into his bright blue eyes.

He brushed it away, and looked around for the beautiful woman who had come between him and the poor old man who had brought him up as his heir.

He saw two ladies in the room.

One of them was quite elderly, and had gray hair crimped beneath a pretty cap.

She wore black silk, and sat on a sofa trifling over a bit of fancy knitting.

"That is Mrs. Carroll," he said to himself. "She is a pretty old lady, though she looks so old and careworn. But she is poor, and that explains it. I dare say I shall grow gray and careworn too when Mrs. St. John takes my uncle's money from me, and I have to earn my bread before I eat it."

He saw another lady standing with her back to him by the piano.

She was *petite* and slender, with a crown of braided black hair, and her robe of rich, wine-colored silk and velvet trailed far behind her on the costly carpet.

She stood perfectly still for a few moments, then turned slowly around, and he saw her face.

"Why, it is Xenie herself!" he exclaimed. "Doctor Shirley lied to me, and I was fool enough to believe his silly joke. Heaven! what I have suffered through my foolish credulity! I've a mind to call Shirley out and shoot him for his atrocity!"

He remained silent a little while studying the lady's dark, beautiful, smiling face, when suddenly he saw the door unclose, and a lady, dressed in the deepest sables of mourning, entered and walked across the floor and sat down by Mrs. Carroll's side upon the sofa.

Howard Templeton started, and a hollow groan broke from his lips.

"My God!" he breathed to himself, "I was mistaken. It is Lora, of course, in that bright-hued dress. How like she is to Xenie! I ought to have remembered that my uncle's wife would be in mourning. Yes, that is Xenie by her mother's side, and Doctor Shirley told me the fatal truth!"

He walked away from the window, and made several hurried turns up and down before the house.

"Shall I go in?" he asked himself. "I know all I came for, now. Yes, I will be fool enough to go in anyhow."

He went up the steps and rang the bell, waiting nervously for the great, carved door to open.

CHAPTER X.

The door swung slowly open, and the gray-haired old servitor whom Howard could remember from childhood, took his card and disappeared down the hallway.

Presently he returned, and informed the young man that the ladies would receive him; and Howard, half regretting, when too late, the hasty impulse that had prompted him enter, was ushered into the drawing-room.

The next moment he found himself returning a stiff, icy bow from his uncle's widow, a half-embarrassed greeting from Mrs. Carroll, and shaking hands with the beautiful Lora, who gave him a shy yet perfectly self-possessed welcome and referred to his visit to the country two years before in a pretty, *naive* way, showing that she remembered him perfectly; although, as she averred, she was little more than a child at the time.

They sat down, and he and Miss Carroll had the talk mostly to themselves, though now and then his glance strayed from her bright, vivacious countenance to the sad, white face of the young widow sitting beside her mother on the sofa, the dark lashes shading her colorless cheeks, a sorrowful droop about her beautiful lips as if her thoughts dwelt on some mournful theme.

Howard had heard people say that she looked ill and pale since Mr. St. John's death, and that after all she must have cared for him a little.

He knew better than that, of course, yet he could not but acknowledge that she played the part of a bereaved wife to perfection.

"It looks like real grief," he said to himself; "but, of course, I know that it is the loss of the money and not the man that weighs her spirits down so heavily."

"You resemble your sister very much, Miss Carroll," he said to Lora, after a little while. "If I were an Irishman, I should say that you look more like your sister than you do like yourself."

The careless, yet odd little speech seemed to have an inexplicable effect upon Lora Carroll. She started violently, her cheeks lost their soft, pink color, the bright smile faded from her lips, and she gave the speaker a keen, half-furtive glance from under her dark-fringed eyelashes.

She tried to laugh, but it sounded forced and unnatural.

Mrs. Carroll, who had been silently listening, broke in carelessly before Lora could speak:

"Yes, indeed, Lora and Xenie are exceedingly like each other, Mr. Templeton. Their aunt, Mrs. Egerton, says that Lora is now the living image of Xenie, when she first came to the city, two years ago."

"I quite agree with her," Mr. Templeton answered, in a light tone, and with a bow to Mrs. Carroll. "The resemblance is very striking."

As he spoke, he moved his chair forward, carelessly yet deliberately, so that he might look into Mrs. St. John's beautiful, pale face.

The young widow did not seem to relish his furtive contemplation. She flushed slightly, and her white hands clasped and unclasped themselves nervously, as they lay folded together in her lap.

She turned her head to one side that she might not encounter the full gaze of his eyes. He smiled to himself at her embarrassment and, turning from her, allowed his gaze to rest upon the bright fire burning behind the polished steel bars of the grate.

A momentary unpleasant silence fell upon them all. Lora broke it after a moment's thought by saying, carelessly, as she opened the piano:

"I remember that you used to sing very well, Mr. Templeton. Won't you favor us now?"

"Lora, my dear," Mrs. Carroll said, in a gently-shocked voice, "you forget that music may not be agreeable to your sister so recently bereaved."

"Oh, Xenie, dear, I beg your pardon," began Lora, turning around, but Mrs. St. John interrupted her by saying, wearily:

"Never mind, mamma, never mind, Lora. I—I—my head aches—I will retire if you will excuse me, and then you may have all the music you wish."

She arose from her seat, gave Mr. Templeton a chill, little bow which he returned as coldly, then went slowly from the room, trailing her sable robes behind her like a pall.

"As cold as ice, by Jove," was Howard's mental comment; "yet she did not appear particularly elated over her prospective triumph. Strange!"

He crossed over to the piano where Lora was restlessly turning over some sheets of music.

"Won't you sing to me, Miss Carroll?" he asked, in a soft, alluring voice.

Lora sat down on the music-stool and laughed as she ran her white fingers over the pearl keys.

"Excuse me—I do not sing," she said, carelessly. "But I will play your accompaniment if you will select a song."

"You do not sing," he said, as he began to turn over the music. "Ah! there is one point at least in which you do not resemble your sister. Mrs. St. John has a very fine voice."

"Yes. Xenie's voice has been well trained," she answered, carelessly; "but I do not care to sing, I would rather hear others."

"How will this please you?" he inquired, selecting a song and laying it up before her.

She glanced at it and answered composedly:

"As well as any. I remember this song. I heard you sing it with Xenie that summer."

"Yes, our voices went well together," he answered, as carelessly. "I wish you would sing it with me now?"

"I cannot, but I will play it for you. Shall we begin now?"

He was silent a moment, looking down at her as she sat there with down-drooped eyes, the gleam of the firelight and gaslight shining on the black braids of her hair and the rich, warm-hued dress that was so very becoming to her dark, bright beauty.

Suddenly he saw something on the white hand that was softly touching the piano keys. He took the slim fingers in his before she was aware.

"Let me see your ring," he said. "It looks familiar. Ah, it is the one I gave you that winter when we——"

She threw back her head and looked at him with wide, angry, black eyes.

"What do you mean?" she said imperiously. "Are you crazy, Mr. Templeton? It is the ring you gave Xenie, certainly, but not me!"

"Lora, love," said her mother's voice from the sofa, in mild reproval. "Do not be rude to Mr. Templeton."

"Mamma, I don't mean to," said Lora, without turning her head; "but he—he spoke as if I were Xenie."

"I beg your pardon, Miss Carroll," said the offender, with a teasing look in his blue eyes, which she did not see; "I did not mean to offend, but do you know that in talking with you, I constantly find myself under the impression that I am talking to your sister. It is one effect of the wonderful resemblance, I presume."

"Yes, I suppose so," admitted Lora; "but," she continued, in a tone of pretty, girlish pique, "I wish you would try and recollect the difference. I am two years younger than my sister, remember, and so it is not a compliment to be taken for a person older than myself!"

"Of course not," said Mr. Templeton, soothingly; "but it was the ring, please remember, that led me into error this time. You see, I gave it to——"

"Yes, you gave it to Xenie," broke in Lora, promptly and coolly; "yes, I know that, but you see she was tired of it, or rather she did not care for it any more—so she gave it to me."

His face whitened angrily, but he said, with assumed carelessness:

"And you—do you care for it, Miss Carroll?"

She lifted her hand and looked at the flashing ruby with a smile.

"Yes, I like it. It is very handsome, and must have cost a large sum of money—more than I ever saw, probably, at one time in my life, I suppose, for I am poor, as you know."

"I thought we were going to have some music, Lora," exclaimed Mrs. Carroll, gasping audibly over her knitting. "You weary Mr. Templeton with your idle talk."

"He began it, mamma," said Lora, carelessly. "Well, Mr. Templeton, I'm going to begin the accompaniment. Get ready."

She touched the keys with skillful fingers, waking a soft, melancholy prelude, and Howard sang in his full, rich, tenor voice:

"'Hapless doom of woman happy in betrothing!Beauty passes like a breath, and love is lost in loathing;Low, my lute; speak low, my lute, but say the world is nothing—Low, lute, low!

"'Love will hover round the flowers when they first awaken;Love will fly the fallen leaf, and not be overtaken;Low, my lute! oh, low, my lute! we fade and are forsaken—Low, dear lute, low!'"

"The poet has very happily blended truth and poesy in that very pathetic song," remarked Lora, with a touch of careless scorn in her voice, as the rich notes ceased. "Well, Mr. Templeton, will you try another song?"

"No, thank you, Miss Carroll—I must be going. I have already trespassed upon your time and patience."

Lora did not gainsay the assertion.

She rose with an almost audible sigh of relief, and stood waiting for him to say good-night.

"May I come and see you again?" he asked, as he bowed over the delicate hand that wore his ruby ring.

"I—we—that is, mamma and I—are going away soon. It may not—perhaps—be convenient for us to receive you again," stammered Lora, hesitating and blushing like the veriest school-girl.

"Ah! I am sorry," he said; "well, then, good-night, and good-bye."

He shook hands with both, holding Lora's hand a trifle longer than necessary, then courteously turned away.

When he was gone, the beautiful girl knelt down by her mother and lifted her flushed and brilliant face with a look of inquiry upon it.

"Well, mamma?" she questioned, gravely.

Mrs. Carroll smiled encouragingly.

"My dear, you acted splendidly," she said, "and so did your sister. I was afraid at first. I thought you were wrong to admit him. It was a terrible test, for the eyes of hatred are even keener than those of love. I trembled for you at first, but you stood the trial nobly. He was completely hoodwinked. No fear now. If you could blind Howard Templeton to the truth, there can be no trouble with the rest of the world."

"And yet once or twice I was terribly frightened," said the girl musingly. "The looks he gave me, the tones of his voice, sometimes his very words, made me tremble with fear. It was, as you say, a terrible test, but I am glad now that I risked it, for I believe that I have succeeded in blinding him. All goes well with us, mamma. Doctor Shirley and Howard Templeton have been completely deceived. The rest will be very easy of accomplishment."

CHAPTER XI.

Thanks to the gossiping tongue of old Doctor Shirley, the interesting news regarding Mrs. St. John speedily became a widespread and accepted fact in society.

It was quite a nine days' wonder at first, and in connection with its discussion a vast deal of speculation was indulged in regarding the possible future of Mr. Howard Templeton, the fair and gilded youth whose heritage might soon be wrested from him, leaving him to battle single-handed with the world.

Before people had stopped wondering over it, Mrs. Egerton added her quota to the excitement by the information that her niece, Mrs. St. John, had gone abroad, taking her mother and sister with her.

She had wanted Lora with *her* that season—she had long ago promised Mrs. Carroll to give Lora a season in the city—but the girl was so wild over the idea of travel that Xenie had taken her with her for company, acting on the advice of Doctor Shirley, who declared that change of scene and cheerful company were actually essential to the preservation of the young invalid's life.

The old doctor, when people interrogated him, confirmed Mrs. Egerton's assertion.

He said that Mrs. St. John had fallen into a state of depression and melancholy so deep as to threaten her health and even her life.

He had advocated an European tour as the most likely means of rousing her from her grief and restoring her cheerful spirits, and she had taken him at his word and gone.

So when Howard Templeton, who had gone down into the country on a little mysterious mission of his own the day after his visit to Lora Carroll, returned to the city, he was electrified by the announcement that Mrs. St. John, with her mother and sister, had sailed for Europe two days previous.

Howard was unfeignedly surprised and confounded at the news.

His face was a study for a physiognomist as he revolved it in his mind.

He went to his private room, ensconced himself in the easiest chair, elevated his feet several degrees higher than his head, and with his fair, clustering locks and bright, blue eyes half obscured in a cloud of cigar smoke, tried to digest the astonishing fact which he had just learned.

It did not take him long to do so.

The brain beneath the white brow and fair, clustering curls was a very clear and lucid one.

He sprang to his feet at last, and said aloud:

"How clever she is, to be sure! It is the most natural thing in the world and the easiest way of carrying out her daring scheme. How perfectly it will smooth over everything."

He walked up and down the richly carpeted room in his blue Turkish silk dressing-gown, his dark brows drawn together in a thoughtful frown, the lights and shades of conflicting feelings faithfully mirrored on his fair and handsome face.

"Why not?" he said, aloud, presently, as if discussing some vexed problem with his inner consciousness. "Why not? I have as good a right to follow as she had to go. I need have no compunctions about spending Uncle John's money. The stroke of fate has not fallen yet. The fabled sword of Damocles hangs suspended over my head, still it may never fall. And in the meantime, why shouldn't I enjoy an European tour? I will, by Jove, I'll follow my Lady Lora by the next steamer. And then—ah, then—checkmate my lady."

He laughed grimly, and nodded at his full length reflection in the long pier-glass at the end of the room.

Then after that moment of exultation a different mood seemed to come over him. His handsome face became grave and even sad.

Throwing himself down carelessly upon a luxurious divan, he took up a volume of poetry lying near and tried to lose himself in its pages.

"Alas! how easily things go wrong, A sigh too much or a kiss too long—And there follows a mist and a blushing rain,And life is never the same again."

He read the words out moodily, then threw the book down impatiently upon the floor.

"These foolish poets!" he said, half-angrily. "They seem always to be aiming at the sore spots in a fellow's heart. How they rake over the ashes of a dead love and strew them along one's path. Love! how strange the word sounds now, when I hate *her* so bitterly!"

CHAPTER XII.

"Darling, how beautiful the sea is. Look how the sun sparkles on the emerald waves, like millions and millions of the brightest diamonds."

Poor little Lora, sitting in the easy-chair on the wide veranda of the little ornate cottage, a forlorn little figure in the deepest of sables, looked up in her sister's face an instant, then burst into a passion of bitter tears.

"The sea, the sea," she moaned despairingly. "Oh! why did you bring me here? I hate the sight and the sound of it! Oh! my poor Jack! my poor Jack!"

Mrs. St. John and Mrs. Carroll exchanged compassionate yet troubled glances, and the latter said gently, yet remonstratingly:

"My dear, my dear, indeed you must not give up to your feelings on every occasion like this. In your weak state of health it is positively dangerous to allow such excitement."

"I don't care, I don't care," wept Lora wildly, hiding her convulsed face against Xenie's compassionate breast. "My heart is broken! I have nothing left to live for, and I wish that I were dead!"

"Darling, let me lead you in. Perhaps if you will lie down and rest you will feel better in both body and mind," said Mrs. St. John, in the gentle, pitying accents used to a sick child.

Lora arose obediently, and leaning on Xenie's arm, was led into her little, airy, white-hung chamber. There her sister persuaded her to lie down upon a lounge while she hovered about her, rendering numberless gentle little attentions, and talking to her in soft, soothing tones.

"Xenie, you are so kind to me," said the invalid, looking at her sister, with a beam of gratitude shining in her large, tearful, dark eyes.

"It is a selfish kindness after all, though, my darling," said Mrs. St. John, gently, "for you know I expect a great reward for what I have done for you. My sisterly duty and my own selfish interest have gone hand-in-hand in this case."

A bright, triumphant smile flashed over her beautiful features as she spoke, and the invalid, looking at her, sighed wearily.

"Xenie," she said, half-hesitatingly, "do not be angry, dear, but I wish you would give up this wild passion of revenge that possesses you. I lie awake nights thinking of it and of my troubles, and I feel more and more that it will be a dreadful deception. Are you not afraid?"

"Afraid of what?" inquired her sister, with a little, impatient ring in the clear, musical tones of her voice.

"Afraid of—of being found out," said Lora, sinking her voice to the faintest whisper.

"There is not the least danger," returned her sister, confidently. "We have managed everything so cleverly there will never be the faintest clew even if the ruse were ever suspected, which it will never be, for who would dream of such a thing? Lora, my dear little sister, I would do much for you, but don't ask me to give up my revenge upon Howard Templeton. I hate him so for his despicable cowardice that nothing on earth would tempt me to forego the sweetness of my glorious vengeance."

"Yet once you loved him," said Lora, with a grave wonder in her sad, white face.

She stared and flushed at Lora's gently reproachful words.

She remembered suddenly that someone else had said those words to her in just the same tone of wonder and reproach.

The night of her short-lived triumph came back into her mind—that brilliant bridal-night when she and Howard Templeton had declared war against each other—war to the knife.

"Yes, once I loved him," she said, with a tone of bitter self-scorn. "But listen to me, Lora. Suppose Jack had treated you as Howard Templeton did me?"

"Jack could not have done it; he loved me too truly," said Lora, lifting her head in unconscious pride.

"You are right, Lora, Jack Mainwaring could not have done it. Few men could have been so base," said Xenie, bitterly. "But, Lora, dear, suppose he *had* treated you so cruelly—mind, I only say suppose—should you not have hated him for it, and wanted to make his heart ache in return?"

Lora was silent a moment. The beautiful young face, so like Xenie's in outline and coloring, so different in its expression of mournful despair, took on an expression of deep tenderness and gentleness as she said, at length:

"No Xenie, I could not have hated Jack even if he had acted like Mr. Templeton. I am very poor-spirited perhaps; but I believe if Jack had treated me so I might have hated the sin, but I could not have helped loving the sinner."

"Ah, Lora, you do not know how you would have felt in such a case. You have been mercifully spared the trial. Let us drop the subject," answered Xenie, a little shortly.

Lora sighed wearily and turned her head away, throwing her black-bordered handkerchief over her face.

Her sister stood still a moment, watching the quiet, recumbent figure, then went to the window, and, drawing the lace curtains aside, stood silently looking out at the beautiful sea, with the sunset glories reflected in the opalescent waves, the soft, spring breeze fluttering the silken rings of dark hair that shaded her broad, white brow.

As she stood there in the soft sunset light in her bright young beauty and rich attire, a smile of proud triumph curved her scarlet lips.

"Ah, Howard Templeton," she mused, "the hour of my triumph is close at hand."

And then, in a gentler tone, while a shade of anxiety clouded her face, she added:

"But poor little Lora! Pray God all may go well with her!"

The roseate hues of sunset faded slowly out, and the purple twilight began to obscure everything.

One by one the little stars sparkled out and took their wonted places in the bright constellations of Heaven.

Still Xenie remained motionless at the window, and still Lora lay quietly on her couch, her pale, anguished young face hidden beneath the mourning handkerchief.

Her sister turned around once and looked at her, thinking she was asleep.

But suddenly in the darkness that began to pervade the room, Xenie caught a faint and smothered moan of pain.

Instantly she hurried to Lora's side.

"My dear, are you in pain?" she said.

Lora raised herself and looked at Xenie's anxious face.

"I—oh, yes, dear," she said, in a frightened tone; "I am ill. Pray go and send mother to me."

Mrs. St. John pressed a tender kiss on the pain-drawn lips and hurried out to seek her mother.

She found her in the little dining-room of the cottage laying the cloth and making the tea. She looked up with a gentle, motherly smile.

"My dear, you are hungry for your tea—you and Lora, I expect," she said. "I let the maid go home to stay with her ailing mother to-night, and promised to make the tea myself. It will be ready now in a minute. Is Lora asleep?"

"Lora is ill, mamma. I will finish the tea, and you must go to her," said Xenie, with a quiver in her low voice, as she took the cloth from her mother's hand.

"Lora sick?" said Mrs. Carroll. "Well, Xenie, I rather expected it. I will go to her. Never mind about the tea, dear, unless you want some yourself."

She bustled out, and Xenie went on mechanically setting the tea-things on the little round table, scarcely conscious of what she was doing, so heavy was her heart.

She loved her sister with as fond a love as ever throbbed in a sister's breast and Lora's peril roused her sympathies to their highest pitch.

Finishing her simple task at last, she filled a little china cup with fragrant tea and carried it to the patient's room.

Mrs. Carroll had enveloped Lora in her snowy embroidered night-robe, and she lay upon the bed looking very pale and preternaturally calm to Xenie's excited fancy.

She drank a little of the tea, then sent Xenie away with it, telling her that she felt quite easy then.

"Go and sit on the veranda as usual, my dear," Mrs. Carroll said, kindly. "I will sit with Lora myself."

"You will call me if I am needed?" asked Mrs. St. John, hesitating on the threshold.

"Yes, dear."

So Xenie went away very sad and heavy-hearted, as if the burden of some intangible sorrow rested painfully upon her oppressed and aching heart.

CHAPTER XIII.

Xenie sat down in the easy-chair on the veranda and looked out at the mystical sea spread out before her gaze, with the moon and stars mirrored in its restless bosom.

Everything was very still. No sound came to her ears save the restless beat of the waves upon the shore. She leaned forward with her arms folded on the veranda rail, and her chin in the hollow of one pink palm, gazing directly forward with dark eyes full of heavy sadness and pain.

She was tired and depressed. Lora had been ill and restless for many nights past, and Xenie and Mrs. Carroll had kept alternate vigils by her sleepless couch.

The last night had been Xenie's turn, and now the strange, narcotic influence of her grief for Lora combined with physical weariness to weigh her eyelids down.

After an interval of anxious listening for sounds from the sick-room, her heavy head dropped wearily on her folded arms, and she fell asleep.

Sleeping, she dreamed. It seemed to her that Howard Templeton, whom once she loved so madly, whom now she bitterly hated, came to her side, and looking down upon her in the sweet spring moonlight, laid his hand upon her and said, gravely, and almost imploringly:

"Xenie, this is the turning-point in your life. Two paths lay before you. Choose the right one and all will go well with you. Peace and happiness will be yours. But choose the evil path and the finger of scorn will one day be pointed at you so that you will not dare to lift your eyes for shame."

In her dream Xenie thought that she threw off her enemy's hand with scorn and loathing.

Then it seemed to her that he gathered her up in his arms and was about to cast her into the deep, terrible sea, when she awoke with a great start, and found herself struggling in the arms of her mother, who had lifted her out of the chair, and was saying, impatiently:

"Xenie, Xenie! child, wake up. You will get your death of cold sleeping out here in the damp night air, and the wind and moisture from the sea blowing over you."

Xenie shook herself free from her mother's grasp, and looked around her for her deadly foe, so real had seemed her dream.

But she saw no tall, proud, manly form, no handsome, blonde face gazing down upon her as she looked.

There was only the cold, white moonlight lying in silvery bars on the floor, and her mother still shaking her by the arm.

"Xenie, Xenie, wake up," she reiterated. "Here I have been shaking and shaking you, and all in vain. You slept like the dead."

"Mamma, I was dreaming," said Mrs. St. John, coming back to herself with a start. "What is the matter? What is the matter? Is my sister worse?"

Mrs. Carroll took her daughter's hand and drew her inside the hallway, then shut and locked the door.

"No, Xenie," she said, abruptly, "Lora is not worse—she is better. Are you awake? Do you know what I am saying? Lora has a beautiful son."

"Oh, mamma, it was but a minute ago that I went out on the veranda."

Mrs. Carroll laughed softly.

"Oh, no, my dear. It was several hours ago. You have been asleep a long time. It is nearly midnight."

"And Lora really has a son, mamma?"

"Yes, Xenie: the finest little fellow I ever saw."

"You promised to call me if she became worse and you needed me," said Mrs. St. John, reproachfully.

"I did not need you, dear. I did everything for Lora my own self," said Mrs. Carroll, with a sort of tender pride in her voice.

"And she is doing well? I may see her—and the baby—my little son!" exclaimed Xenie, with a sudden ring of triumph in her voice.

"Yes, she is doing well; a little flighty now and then, and very weak; she could not bear the least excitement. But you shall go to her in a minute. She wished it."

They went into the dimly-lighted, quiet room, and Xenie kissed her sister and cried over her very softly. Then she took the bundle of warm flannel out of Lora's arms and uncovered a red and wrinkled little face.

"Why, mamma, you said it was beautiful," she said, disappointedly; "and I am bound to confess that, to me, it looks like a very old and wrinkled little man."

Mrs. Carroll laughed very softly.

"I don't believe you ever met with a very young baby before, my dear," she said. "I assure you he is quite handsome for his age, and he will improve marvelously in a week's time."

Xenie stood still, holding the babe very close and tight in her arms, while a dazzling smile of triumph parted her beautiful scarlet lips. She hated to lay it down, for while she held it warm and living against her breast she seemed to taste the full sweetness of the wild revenge she had planned against her enemy.

"Oh, mamma, Lora," she cried, "how impatiently I have waited for this hour! And now I am so glad, so glad! We will go home soon, now—as soon as our darling is well enough to travel—and then I shall triumph to the uttermost over Howard Templeton."

She kissed the little pink face tenderly and exultantly two or three times, then laid him back half-reluctantly on his mother's impatient arm.

"He is my little son," she whispered, gently; "for you are going to give him to me, aren't you, Lora?"

A weary sigh drifted over the white lips of the beautiful young mother.

"I will lend him to you, Xenie, for I have promised," she murmured; "but, oh, my sister, does it not seem cruel and wrong to take such an innocent little angel as that for the instrument of revenge?"

Xenie drew back, silent and offended.

"Xenie, darling, don't be angry," pleaded Lora's weak and faltering tones; "I will keep my promise. You shall call him yours, and the world shall believe it. He shall even call you mother, but you must let me be near him always—you must let him love me a little, dear, because I am his own dear mother."

She paused a moment, then added, in faint accents:

"And, Xenie, you will call him Jack—for his father's sake, you know."

"Yes, darling," Xenie answered, tenderly, melted out of her momentary resentment by the pathos of Lora's looks and words, "it shall all be as you wish. I only wish to call him mine before the world, you know. I would not take him wholly from you, my little sister."

"A thousand thanks," murmured Lora, feebly, then she put up her white arm and drew Xenie's face down to hers.

"I have been dreaming, dear," she said. "It seemed to me in my dream as if my poor Jack were not dead after all. It seemed to me he escaped from the terrible fire and shipwreck, and came back to me brave and handsome, and loving, as of old. It seems so real to me even now that I feel as though I could go out and almost lay my hand upon my poor boy's head. Ah, Xenie, if it only could be so!"

Mrs. St. John looked across at her mother, and Mrs. Carroll shook her head warningly. Then she said aloud, in a soothing tone:

"These are but sick fancies, dear. You must not think of Jack any more to-night, but of your pretty babe."

"Grandmamma is quite proud of her little grandson already," said Xenie, with tender archness.

"Mamma, shall you really love the little lad? You were so angry at first," Lora said, falteringly.

"That is all over with now, my daughter. I shall love my little grandson as dearly as I love his mother, soon," replied Mrs. Carroll; "but now, love, I cannot allow you to talk any longer. Excitement is not good for you. Run away to bed, Xenie. We do not need you to-night."

"Let me stay and share your vigil," pleaded Xenie.

"No, it is my turn to-night. Last night you sat up, you know. I will steal a little rest upon the lounge when Lora gets composed to sleep again."

Xenie went away to her room and threw herself across the bed, dressed as she was, believing that she was too excited to go to sleep again.

But a gradual drowsiness stole over her tumultuous thoughts, and she was soon wrapped in a troubled, dreamful slumber.

Daylight was glimmering faintly into the room, when Mrs. Carroll rushed in, pale and terrified, and shook her daughter wildly.

"Oh, Xenie, wake, wake, for God's sake!" she cried, in the wildest accents of despair and terror. "Such a terrible, terrible thing has happened to Lora!"

CHAPTER XIV.

Xenie sprang to her feet, broad awake at those fearful words.

"Oh, mamma!" she gasped, in terror-stricken accents, "what is it? My sister—is she worse? Is she——"

She thought of death, but she paused, and could not bring her lips to frame that terrible word, and stood waiting speechlessly, with parted lips and frightened, dark eyes, for her mother to speak.

But Mrs. Carroll, as if that one anguished sentence had exhausted all her powers, fell forward across the bed, her face growing purple, her lips apart in a frantic struggle for breath.

Xenie hurriedly caught up a pitcher of water standing near at hand, and dashed it into her convulsed face, with the quick result of seeing her shiver, gasp, and spring up again.

"Mamma, speak!" she cried, shaking her wildly by the arm; "what has happened to you? What has happened to Lora?"

Mrs. Carroll's eyes, full of a dumb, agonizing terror, turned upon Xenie's wild, white face.

She tried to speak, but the words died chokingly in her throat, and she lifted her hand and pointed toward the door.

Instantly Xenie turned, and rushed from the room.

As she crossed the narrow hallway a breath of the fresh, chilly morning air blew across her face. The door that Mrs. Carroll had securely locked the night before was standing wide open, and the wind from the sea was blowing coolly in.

With a terrible foreboding of some impending calamity, Xenie sprang through the open doorway of Lora's room, and ran to the bed.

Oh! horrors, the bed was empty!

The beautiful young mother and the little babe, the day-star of Xenie's bright hopes, were gone!

Xenie looked around her wildly, but the pretty little chamber was silent and tenantless.

With a cry of fear and dread commingled, she rushed toward the door, and encountered her mother creeping slowly in, like a pallid ghost, in the chilly, glimmering dawn of the new day.

"Oh, mamma, where is Lora?" she cried, in a faint voice, while her limbs seemed to totter beneath her.

Mrs. Carroll shook her head, and put her hands to her throat, while her pallid features seemed to work with convulsive emotion. The terrible shock she had sustained seemed to have stricken her dumb.

"Oh, mamma, mamma, cannot you speak? Cannot you tell me?" implored her daughter.

But by signs and gestures Mrs. Carroll made her understand that the terrible constriction in her throat made it impossible for her to utter a word.

For a moment Mrs. St. John stood still, like a silent statue of despair, but with a sudden inspiration she brought writing materials, placed them on a small table, and said to her mother:

"Sit down, mamma, and write what you know."

Mrs. Carroll's anguished face brightened at the suggestion. She sat down quickly at the little table, and drawing a sheet of paper toward her, dipped the pen into the ink, and began to write.

Xenie leaned over her shoulder, and watched eagerly for the words that were forming beneath her hand.

But, alas, the nervous shock her mother had sustained made her hand tremble like an aspen leaf.

Great, sprawling, blotted, inky characters soon covered the fair sheet thickly, but among them all there was not one legible word.

Xenie groaned aloud in her terrible impatience and pain.

"Oh, mamma, try again!" she wailed. "Write slowly and carefully. Rest your arm upon the table, and let your hand move slowly—very slowly."

And with an impotent moan, Mrs. Carroll took another sheet of paper and tried to subdue her trembling hands to the task for whose fulfillment her daughter was waiting so anxiously.

But again the blotted characters were wholly illegible. No effort of the mother's will could still the nervous, trembling hands, and render legible the anguished words she laboriously traced upon the paper.

She sighed hopelessly as her daughter shook her head.

"Never mind, mamma," she said, "let it go, you are too nervous to form a single letter legibly. I will ask you some questions instead, and you will bow when your answer should be affirmation, and shake your head to indicate the negative."

Mrs. Carroll gave the required token of assent to this proposition.

"Very well. Now I will ask you the first question," said Xenie, trying to subdue her quivering voice into calm accents. "Mamma, did Lora go to sleep after I left you together?"

A shake of the head negatived the question.

"She was restless and flighty, then, perhaps, still dwelling on her dream about her husband?"

This question received an affirmative answer.

"But after awhile she became composed and fell asleep—did she not?" continued Mrs. St. John.

Mrs. Carroll bowed, her lips moving continually in a vain and yearning effort after words.

"And then you lay down upon the lounge to snatch a few minutes of repose?" asserted Xenie.

Again she received an affirmative reply.

"Mamma, did you sleep long?" was the next question.

Mrs. Carroll shook her head with great energy.

"Oh! no, of course you did not!" exclaimed Xenie, quickly, "for it was midnight when I left you, and if Lora was wakeful and restless it must have been several hours before either one fell asleep. And it is not daylight yet, so you must have slept a very little while. Were you awakened by any noise, mamma?"

The question was instantly negatived

"You were nervous and ill at ease, then, and simply awoke of yourself?" continued Mrs. St. John, anxiously.

Mrs. Carroll's earnest, dark eyes said yes almost as plainly as her bowed head.

"And when you woke, Lora and the babe were gone, mamma, and the front door stood wide open—is that the way of it, mamma?" continued Xenie, anxiously watching her mother's face for the confirmation of her question.

Mrs. Carroll gave assent to it while a hoarse wail of anguish issued from her drawn, white lips.

Xenie echoed the wail, and for a moment her white face was hidden in her hands while the most terrible apprehension stabbed her to the heart.

Then she looked up and said quickly:

"She must have wandered away in a momentary fit of flightiness—don't you think so?"

And again Mrs. Carroll gave a quick motion of assent.

"Then I must find her, mamma," said Xenie, quickly. "She cannot have gone very far. She was too weak to get away from us unless—— Oh! my God! she cannot have gone to the water!" moaned Xenie, clasping her hands in horror.

Mrs. Carroll looked as if she were going into a fit at the bare suggestion.

Her face turned purple again, her eyes stared wildly, she clutched at her throat like one choking.

Xenie forced her back upon the lounge, applied restoratives, then exclaimed wildly:

"Mamma, I cannot bear to leave you thus, but I must go and seek for my sister. Even now she may be perishing in reach of our hands. Ninon, the maid, will be here in a little while. She will care for you, and I will bring back my poor little Lora."

She kissed her mother's face as she spoke, then hurried out, shawlless and bare-headed, into the chill morning air.

It was a dark and gloomy dawn, with a drizzle of rain falling steadily through the murky atmosphere.

A fine, white mist was drawn over the sea like a winding sheet. The sun had not tried to rise over the dismal prospect.

Xenie ran heedlessly down the veranda steps, and bent her steps to the seashore, looking about her carefully as she went, and calling frantically all the time:

"Lora, Lora, Lora! Where are you, my darling? Where are you?"

But no answer came to her wild appeal.

The soft, low patter of the steady rain, and the solemn sound of the waves as they madly surged upon the shore, seemed like a funeral requiem in her ears.

She could not bear the awful voice of the sea, for she remembered that Lora had hated it because her husband was buried in its illimitable waves.

But suddenly a faint and startling sound came to her ears.

She thought it was the moan of the wind rising at first, then it sounded again almost at her feet—the shrill, sharp wail of an infant.

Xenie turned around and saw, not twenty paces from her, a little bundle of soft, white flannel lying upon the wet sand.

She ran forward with a scream of joy, and picked it up in her arms, and drew aside one corner of the little embroidered blanket.

Joy, joy! it was Lora's baby—Lora's baby, lying forlorn and deserted on the wet sand with the hungry waves rolling ever nearer and nearer toward it, as though eager to draw it down in their cold and fatal embrace.

With a low murmur of joy, Xenie kissed the cold little face and folded it closely in her arms.

"Lora cannot be very far now," she thought, her heart beating wildly with joy. "She was so weak the babe has slipped from her arms, and she did not know it. She will come back directly to find it."

She ran along the shore, looking through the gray dawn light everywhere for her sister, and calling aloud in tender accents:

"Lora, Lora, my darling!"

But suddenly, as she looked, she saw a strangely familiar form coming toward her along the sand.

It was a man clothed in a gray tweed traveling suit, such as tourists wear abroad.

He stopped with a cry of surprise as they met, and there on the wild shores of France, with the rain beating down on her bare head and thin dress, with Lora's baby tightly clasped in her bare arms, Xenie St. John found herself face to face with her enemy.

CHAPTER XV.

Like one stricken motionless by terror, she stood still and looked up into the proud face and scornful blue eyes of the man she had thought far, far away beneath the skies of his native land.

The ground seemed slipping from beneath her feet, the wild elements seemed whirling aimlessly over her head; she forgot Lora, she forgot the child that nestled against her breast; she remembered nothing else but her enemy's presence and the deadly peril to which her secret was exposed.

"Howard Templeton," she panted forth wildly, "why are you here?"

"Mrs. St. John," he returned, with a bitter smile, "I might rather ask you that question. What are *you* doing here in this stormy dawn, with your bare head and your thin slippers and evening dress? Permit me to offer you my cloak. Do you forget that it is cold and rainy, that you court certain death for yourself and the—the——"

He paused without ending the sentence and looked at the little white bundle lying helpless in her arms, and a steely gleam of hatred flared into his eyes.

"The child," she said, finishing the sentence for him with a passionate quiver of joy in her voice, "*my* child—Howard Templeton—the little one that has come to me to avenge his mother's wrongs. Look at him. This is your uncle's heir, this tiny little babe! He will strip you of every dollar you now hold so unjustly, and his mother's revenge will then be complete."

She turned back a corner of the blanket, and gave him a glimpse of the little pink face, and the babe set up a feeble and pitiful little wail.

It was as though the unconscious little creature repeated its mother's plaintive remonstrance against making such an innocent little angel the instrument for consummating a cruel revenge.

But Xenie was deaf to the voice of conscience, or she might have fancied that its accusing voice spoke loudly in the wail of the little babe.

She looked at Howard Templeton with a glow of triumph in her face, her black eyes shining like stars.

The wind and the rain tossed her dark, loosened ringlets about her, making her look like some mad creature with that wicked glow of anger and revenge in her beautiful, spirited face.

"Say, is it not a glorious revenge?" she cried. "You scorned me because I was poor. I was young, I was fair, I was loving and true, but all that counted for nothing in your eyes. For lack of gold you left me. Did you think my heart would break in silence? Ah, no, I swore to give you back pang for pang, and I have taken from you all that your base heart ever held dear—gold, shining gold. Through me you will be stripped of all. Is it not a brilliant victory? Ha! ha!"

His blue eyes flashed down into her vivid, black ones, giving her hate for hate and scorn for scorn. In a low, concentrated voice, he said:

"Are you not afraid to taunt me thus? Look there at that seething ocean beneath its shroud of mist. Do you see that no one is near? Do you know that there is no one in hearing? Suppose I should take you up with your revenge in your arms and cast you into yonder sea? The opportunity is mine, the temptation is great."

"Yet you will not do it," she answered, giving him a glance of superb scorn.

"Why do you say I will not do it?" he asked; "why should I spare you? You have not spared me! You are trying to wrest my inheritance from me. We are sworn and deadly foes. I have nothing to lose by your death, everything to gain. Why should I not take the present opportunity and sweep you from my path forever?"

He paused and looked down at her in passionate wrath while he wondered what she would say to all this; but she was silent.

"Again I ask you why should I spare you?" he repeated; "are you not afraid of my vengeance, Xenie St. John?"

"No, I am not afraid," she repeated, defiantly, yet even as she spoke he saw that a shudder that was not of the morning's cold shook her graceful form. A sudden consciousness of the truth that lurked in his words had rushed over her.

"Yes, we *are* deadly foes," she repeated to herself, with a deeper consciousness of the meaning of those words than she had ever had before. "Why should he spare me, since I am wholly in his power?"

His voice broke in suddenly on her swift, tumultuous thoughts, making her start with its cold abruptness.

"Ah, I see that you begin to realize your position," he said, icily. "What is your revenge worth now in this moment of your deadly peril? Is it dearer to you than your life?"

"Yes, it is dearer to me than my life," she answered, steadily. "If nothing but my life would buy revenge for me I would give it freely!"

He regarded her a moment with a proud, silent scorn. She returned the gaze with interest, but even in her passionate anger and hatred she could not help owning to her secret heart that she had never seen him looking so handsome as he did just then in the rough but well-fitting tweed suit, with the glow of the morning on his fair face, and that light of scorn in his dark-blue eyes.

Suddenly he spoke:

"Well, go your way, Xenie St. John. You are in my way, but it is not by this means I will remove you from it. I am not a murderer—your life is safe from my vengeance. Yet I warn you not to go further in your wild scheme of vengeance against me. It can only result in disaster to yourself. I am forewarned of your intentions and your wicked plot. You can never wrest from me the inheritance that Uncle John intended for me!"

"We shall see!" she answered, with bold defiance, undaunted by his threatening words.

Then, as the little babe in her arms began to moan pitifully again, she remembered the dreadful trouble that had sent her out into the rain, and turning from him with a sudden wail of grief, she began to run along the shore, looking wildly around for some trace of the lost one.

She heard Howard's footsteps behind her, and redoubled her speed, but in a minute his hand fell on her shoulder, arresting her flight. He spoke hastily:

"I heard you calling for Lora before I met you—speak, tell me if she also is wandering out here like a madwoman, and why?"

She turned on him fiercely.

"What does it matter to you, Howard Templeton?"

"If she is lost I can help you to find her," he retorted. "What can you do? A frail woman wandering in the rain with a helpless babe in your arms!"

Bitterly as she hated him, an overpowering sense of the truth of his words rushed over her.

She hated that he should help her and yet she could not let her own angry scruples stand in the way of finding Lora.

She looked up at him and the hot tears brimmed over in her black eyes and splashed upon her white cheeks.

"Lora is missing," she answered, in a broken voice. "She has been ill, and last night she wandered in her mind. This morning while mamma and I slept she must have stolen away in her delirium. Mamma was prostrated by the shock, and I came out alone to find her."

"You should have left the child at home. It will perish in the rain and cold," he said, looking at her keenly.

She shivered and grew white as death, but pressed the babe closer to her breast that the warmth of her own heart might protect its tender life.

"Why did you bring the child?" he persisted, still watching her keenly.

"I will not tell you," she answered, defiantly, but with a little shiver of dread. What if he had seen her when she found it on the sands?

"Very well; you shall not stay out longer with it, at least. Granted that we are deadly foes—still I have a man's heart in my breast. I would not willingly see a woman perish. Go home, Xenie, and care for your mother. I will undertake the search for Lora. If I find her you shall know it immediately. I promise you."

He took the heavy cloak from his own shoulders and fastened it around her shivering form.

She did not seem to notice the action, but stood still mechanically, her dark, tearful eyes fixed on the mist-crowned sea. He followed her gaze, and said in a quick tone of horror:

"You do not believe she is in there? It would be too horrible!"

"Oh, my God!" Mrs. St. John groaned, with a quiver of awful dread in her voice.

He shivered through all his strong, lithe young frame. The thought of such a death was terrible to him.

"You said she was ill and delirious?" he said, abruptly.

"Yes," she wailed.

"Poor Lora—poor little Lora!" he exclaimed, with a sudden tone of pity. "Alas! is it not too probable that she has met her death in those fatal waves?"

"Oh, she could not, she could not," Xenie moaned, wildly. "She hated the sea. Her lover was drowned in it. She could not bear the sight or the sound of it."

He did not answer for a moment. He was looking away from her with a great, solemn dread and pity in his beautiful, blue eyes. Suddenly he said, abruptly:

"Go home, Mrs. St. John, and stay there until you hear news. I will go and arouse the village. I will have help in the search, and if she is found we will bring her home. If she is not, God help you, for I fear she has drowned herself in the sea."

With a long, moaning cry of anguish, Xenie turned from him and sped along the wet sand back to her mother. Howard Templeton watched the flying figure on its way with a grave trouble in his handsome face, and when she was out of sight, he turned in an opposite direction and walked briskly along the sand, looking carefully in every direction.

"They talk of judgment," he muttered. "Has God sent this dreadful thing upon Xenie St. John for her sinful plans? If it is so, surely it will bring her to repentance. In the face of such a terrible affliction, she must surely be afraid to persist in attempting such a stupendous fraud."

CHAPTER XVI.

Half dead with weariness and sorrow, Mrs. St. John staggered into her mother's presence with the wailing infant in her arms.

She sank down upon the floor by the side of the couch and laid the child on her mother's breast, moaning out:

"I found him down there, lying on the wet sand all alone, mamma—all alone! Oh! Lora, Lora!"

A heart-rending moan broke from Mrs. Carroll's lips. Her face was gray and death-like in the chill morning light.

She closed her arms around the babe and strained it fondly to her breast.

"Mamma, are you better? Can you speak yet? I have much to tell you," said Xenie, anxiously.

Mrs. Carroll made a violent effort at articulation, then shook her head, despairingly.

"I will send for the doctor as soon as the maid returns. She cannot be long now—it is almost broad daylight," said Xenie, with a heavy sigh. "And in the meantime I will feed the babe. It is cold and hungry. Mamma, shall I give it a little milk and water, warmed and sweetened?"

Mrs. Carroll assented, and Xenie went out into the little kitchen, lighted a fire and prepared the infant's simple nourishment.

Returning to Lora's room, she sat down in a low rocker, took the child in her arms, and carefully fed it from a teaspoon, first removing the cold blanket from around it, and wrapping it in warm, dry flannels.

Its fretful wails soon ceased under her tender care, and it fell into a gentle slumber on her breast.

"Now, mamma," she said, as she rocked the little sleeper gently to and fro, "I will tell you what happened to me while I was searching for my sister."

In as few words as possible, she narrated her meeting with Howard Templeton.

Mrs. Carroll greeted the information with a groan. She was both astonished and frightened at his appearance in France, when they had supposed him safe in America.

She struggled for speech so violently that the dreadful hysteric constriction in her throat gave way before her mental anguish, and incoherent words burst from her lips.

"Oh, Xenie, he will know all now, and Lora's good name and your own scheme of revenge will be equally and forever blasted! All is lost!"

"No, no, mamma, that shall never be! He shall not find us out. I swear it!" exclaimed her daughter passionately. "Let him peep and pry as he will, he shall not learn anything that he could prove. We have managed too cleverly for that."

And then the next moment she cried out:

"But, oh, mamma, you are better—you can speak again!"

"Yes, thank Heaven!" breathed Mrs. Carroll, though she articulated with difficulty, and her voice was hoarse and indistinct. "But, Xenie, what could have brought Howard Templeton here? Can he suspect anything? Did he know that we were here?"

Xenie was silent for a moment, then she said, thoughtfully:

"It may be that he vaguely suspects something wrong. Indeed, from some words he used to me, I believe he did. But what then? It is perfectly impossible that he could prove any charge he might make, so it matters little what he suspects. Oh, mamma, you should have seen how black, how stormy he looked when I showed him the child, and told him it was mine. I should have felt so happy then had it not been for my fear and dread over Lora."

"My poor girl—my poor Lora!" wailed the stricken mother. "Oh, Xenie, I am afraid she has cast herself into the sea."

"Oh, no, do not believe it. She did not, she could not! You know how she hated the sea. She has but wandered away, following her wild fancy of finding her husband. She was too weak to go far. They will soon find her and bring her back," said Xenie, trying to whisper comfort to the bereaved heart of the mother, though her own lay heavy as lead in her breast.

She rose after a moment and went to the window.

"It is strange that Ninon does not return to get the breakfast," she said, looking out. "Can her mother be worse, do you think, mamma?"

"She may be, but I hardly think it likely. She was better of the fever the last time Ninon went to see her. It is likely that the foggy, rainy morning has deceived her as to the lateness of the hour. She will be along presently, no doubt," said Mrs. Carroll, carelessly; for her trouble rendered her quite indifferent to her bodily comfort.

Xenie sat down again, and rocked the babe silently for a little while.

"Oh, mamma, how impatient I grow!" she said, at length. "It seems to me I cannot wait longer. I must put the child down and go out again. I cannot bear this dreadful suspense."

"No, no; I will go myself," said Mrs. Carroll, struggling up feebly from the lounge. "You are cold and wet now, my darling. You will get your death out there in the rain. I must not lose both my darlings at once."

But Xenie pushed her back again with gentle force.

"No, mamma, you shall not go—you are already ill," she said. "Let the child lie in your arms, and I will go to the door and see if anyone is coming."

Filled with alternate dread and hope, she went to the door and looked out.

No, there was naught to be seen but the rain and the mist—nothing to be heard but the hollow moan of the ocean, or the shrill, piping voice of the sea birds skimming across the waves.

"It is strange that the maid does not come," she said again, oppressed with the loneliness and brooding terror around her.

She sat down again, and waited impatiently for what seemed a considerable time; then she sprang up restlessly.

"Mamma, I will just walk out a very little way," she said. "I must see if anyone is coming yet."

"You must not go far, then, Xenie." Mrs. Carroll remonstrated.

Xenie dashed out into the rain again, and ran recklessly along the path, looking far ahead of her as if to pierce the mystery that lay beyond her.

Presently she saw a young French girl plodding along toward her.

It was Ninon, the belated maid. Over her arm she carried a dripping-wet shawl.

It was a pretty shawl, of warm woolen, finely woven, and striped with broad bars of white and red.

Xenie knew it instantly, and a cry of terror broke from her lips. It belonged to Lora.

She had seen it lying around her sister's shoulders when she kissed her good-night; yet here it hung on Ninon's arms, wet and dripping, the thick, rich fringes all matted with seaweed.

CHAPTER XVII.

Xenie's heart beat so fast at the sight of what Ninon was carrying that she could not move another step.

She had to stand still with her hands clasped over her throbbing side and wait till the girl came up to her. Then:

"Oh, Heaven, Ninon, where did you get that?" she gasped, looking at the shawl with eyes full of horror, yet afraid to touch it, for it seemed like some dead thing.

"Oh, ma'amselle," faltered the girl stopping short and looking at Xenie's anguished face. "Oh, ma'amselle," she faltered again, and her pretty, piquant face grew white and her black eyes sought the ground, for Ninon, although poor and lowly, had a very tender heart, and she could not bear to see the anguish in the eyes of her young mistress.

"I asked you where did you get that shawl?" Xenie repeated. "It was my sister's shawl. She wore it last night, and now, to-day, she is missing. Did you know that, Ninon?"

"Yes," the girl answered, in her pretty, broken English. She had heard it. A gentleman, a tourist, had brought the news to the village, and the men were all out looking for her.

Would her mistress come to the house? She had something to tell her, but not out there in the cold and wet. She looked fit to drop, indeed she did, declared the voluble, young French girl.

So she half-led, half-dragged Mrs. St. John back to the cottage and into the room where the stricken mother was waiting for tidings of her lost one.

The maid had a sorrowful story to tell.

The waves had cast a dead body up on the beach an hour ago—the corpse of a woman, thinly dressed in white, with long, beautiful black hair flowing loosely and tangled with seaweed.

They could not tell who she was, for—and here Ninon shuddered visibly—the rough waves had battered and swollen her features utterly beyond recognition.

But they thought that she was young, for her limbs were white and round, and beautifully moulded, and this shawl which Ninon carried had been tightly fastened about her shoulders.

The maid had recognized it and brought it with her to show the bereaved mother and sister, and to ask if they wished to go and view the body and try to identify it.

All this the maid told sorrowfully and hesitatingly, while the two women sat like statues and listened to her, every vestige of hope dying out of their hearts at the pitiful story, and at length Xenie cast herself down upon the wet shawl and wept and wailed over it as though it had been the dead body of poor Lora herself lying there all wet and dripping with the ocean spray before her anguished sight.

Then Ninon begged her to listen to what she had to say further.

"The gentleman is going to send a vehicle for you that you may go and see the body, if you wish—I can hear the roll of the wheels now! Shall I help you to get ready?"

Xenie looked at her mother with a dumb inquiry on her beautiful, pallid features.

"Yes, go, dear, if you can bear it. Perhaps, after all, it may not be our darling," said Mrs. Carroll, with a heavy sigh, even while she tried to cheat her heart by the doubt which she felt to be a vain one.

So, with Ninon's aid, Xenie changed her wet and drabbled garments for a plain, black silk dress, and a black hat and thick veil.

Then, leaving the maid to take care of her mother, Mrs. St. John entered the vehicle and was driven to the place where a group of excited villagers kept watch over a ghastly something upon the sand—the mutilated semblance of a human being that the cruel sea had beaten and buffeted beyond recognition.

It was a terrible ordeal for that young, beautiful, and loving sister to pass alone.

As she stepped from the vehicle with a wildly-beating heart before the curious scrutiny of the strangers around her, she involuntarily cast a glance around her in the vague, scarce-defined belief that Howard Templeton would be upon the scene. But, no, there was no sign of his presence.

Strangers advanced to lead her forward; strangers questioned her; strangers drew back the sheet that had been reverently folded over the dead, and showed her that ghastly form that all believed must have been her sister.

She knelt down, trying to keep back her sobs, and looked at the form lying there in the awful majesty of death, with the cold, drizzling rain beating down on its swollen, discolored features.

How could that awful thing be Lora—her own, beautiful, tender Lora?

And yet, and yet, that beautiful, long, black hair—that fine, embroidered night-robe, hanging in tattered remnants now where the sea had rent it—did they not belong to her sister? Sickening with an awful dread, she touched one of the cold, white hands.

It was a ghastly object now, swollen and livid, yet you could see that once it had been a beautiful hand, delicate, dimpled, tapering.

And on the slender, third finger, deeply imbedded in the swollen flesh, were two rings—plain, broad, gold bands. Xenie's eyes fell upon them, and with a wild, despairing cry, "Oh, Lora, my sister!" she fell upon the wet sand, in a deep and death-like swoon.

CHAPTER XVIII.

After leaving Xenie on the seashore, Howard Templeton walked away hurriedly to the little fishing village, a mile distant, and gave the alarm of Lora's disappearance.

By a promise of large rewards, he speedily induced a party of men to set out in separate directions to scour the adjacent country for the wanderer.

But scarcely had they set out on their mission when someone brought to Howard the news of the corpse that old ocean had cast upon the sands.

Dreading, yet fully expecting to behold the dead body of Lora Carroll, Howard Templeton turned back and accompanied the man to the scene.

They found a group of excited men and women gathered, on the shore, drawn thither by that nameless fascination which the dreadful and mysterious always possesses for every class of minds whether high or low.

Conspicuous in the group was Ninon, the pretty young maid-servant, and, as Howard came upon the scene, she was volubly explaining to the bystanders that the shawl which was tightly pinned about the shoulders of the dead woman belonged to the missing girl for whom the men had gone out to search.

Was she quite sure of it, they asked her. Yes, she was quite sure.

She had seen it night after night lying across the bed in the young lady's sleeping-apartment.

When she was ill and restless, as often happened, she would put it around her shoulders and walk up and down the room for hours, weeping and wringing her hands like one in sore distress.

"Yes," Ninon said, she could swear to the shawl. She would take it home with her and show it to her mistress, and they would see that she was right.

No one interfered to prevent her.

With an irrepressible shudder at touching the dead, the girl drew out the pins and took the wet shawl.

Then, as she started on her homeward way, Howard Templeton, who had stood still like one in a dream of horror, started forward and told her that he himself would send a vehicle for the ladies, that they might come if they wished to identify the body.

For himself, he had no idea whether or not that the poor, bruised and battered corpse could be Lora Carroll.

He could see nothing that reminded him of her except the beautiful, black hair lying about her head in heavy, clinging masses, sodden with water and tangled with seaweed.

He longed, yet dreaded, for Mrs. Carroll and her daughter to arrive and confirm or dissipate his fears and end the dreadful suspense.

And yet, with the rumble of the departing wheels of the conveyance he had sent for them, a sudden cowardice stole over the young man's heart.

He could not bear the thought of the anguish of which he might soon be the witness.

Obeying a sudden, inexplicable impulse, he turned from the little company of watchers by the dead and walked off from them, taking the course along the shore that led away from the little village.

Oftentimes those simple little impulses that seem to us mere accidental happenings, would appear in reality to be the actual fulfillment of some divine design.

Howard little dreamed, as he turned away with a kind of sick horror, that was no shame to his manhood, from the sight of so much misery, that "a spirit in his feet" was guiding him straight to the living Lora, even while his heart foreboded that it was she who lay cold and lifeless on the ocean shore.

Yet so it was. True it is, as the great bard expresses it, that "there's a divinity that shapes our ends, rough-hew them as we will."

Howard hurried along aimlessly, his thoughts so busy on one painful theme that he took no note of where he was going, or how fast he went.

He was a rapid walker usually, and when he at length brought himself to a sudden abrupt stop he realized with a start that he had come several miles at least.

The rain had ceased, the sun had come out in all its majestic glory, and beneath its fervid kisses the mist that hid the ocean was melting into thin air.

It bade fair to be a beautiful day, after all.

The pearly rain-drops sparkled like diamonds on the leaves and flowers, the sky was blue and beautiful, with here and there a little white cloud sailing softly past.

The day had began like many a life, in clouds and tears, but it promised to close in as fair and sweet a serenity as many an early-shadowed life has done.

Howard involuntarily thought of the poet's beautiful lines:

"Be still, sad heart, and cease repining,Behind the clouds is the sun still shining!Days of sunshine are given to all,Though into each life some rain must fall."

He paused and looked around him. He found that he had come into the outskirts of another rude, little fishing village.

A little ahead of him he could see the fishers bustling about on the shore.

"I have come four miles, at least," he said to himself. "What a great, hulking, cowardly fellow I am to run that far from a woman's tears. Far better have stayed and tried to dry them. Um! She wouldn't have let me," he added, with a rueful second thought.

Then, after a moment's idle gazing out at sea, aimlessly noting the flash of a sea-gull's wing as it wheeled in the blue air above him, he said, resolutely:

"I'll go back, anyhow. Perhaps I can do something to help them. They are but women—my countrywomen, too, and I'll not desert them in their trouble, even though *she* does hate me."

He turned around suddenly to return, and the fate that was watching him to prevent such a thing, placed a simple stone in the way. He stepped upon it heedlessly, his ankle turned, and, with a sharp cry of pain, Howard fell to the ground.

He made an effort to rise, but the acute pains that suddenly darted through his ankle caused him to fall back upon the wet sand in a hurry.

"Umph! my ankle is evidently master of the situation," he thought, with an expression of comical distress.

Raising himself on his elbow, he shouted aloud to the men in the distance, and presently two of them came running to his assistance.

"I have sprained my ankle," he explained to them in their native tongue. "Please assist me to rise, and I will try to walk."

But when they took him by the arms and raised him up, they found that it was impossible for him to walk.

"This is a deuced bore at the present time, certainly," complained the sufferer. "Can you get me any kind of a trap to drive me back to the village yonder?"

The peasants looked at him stupidly, and informed him carelessly that there was nothing of the kind available. Only one man in the vicinity owned a horse, and it had sickened and died a week before.

Howard felt a great and exceeding temptation to swear a very small oath at this crisis, but being too much of a gentleman to yield to this wicked whisper of the evil one, groaned very loudly instead.

"Then what the deuce am I to do?" he inquired, as much of himself as of the two fishermen. "How am I to get away from this spot of wet sand? Where am I to go?"

The peasants scrutinized him as stupidly as before, and to all of these questions answered flatly that they did not know, indeed.

Howard thought within himself that the proverbial politeness of the French was greatly tempered by stupidity in this case.

"Well, then," he inquired next, "is there any kind of a hotel around here?"

"Yes, there was such a place," they informed him, readily; and Howard at once begged them to summon aid and construct a litter for him, promising to reward them liberally if they would carry him to the hotel.

Gold—that magic "open sesame" to every heart—procured him ready and willing attention.

It was but a short while before he found himself in tolerably comfortable quarters at the rude hotel of the fishing village, and obsequiously waited upon by the single Esculapius the place afforded.

Howard's sprain was pronounced very severe indeed. It was so painful that he could not walk upon it at all, and was ordered to strict confinement to his couch for three days.

"A fine prospect, by Jove!" Howard commented, discontentedly. "What am I to do shut up here three days in solitary confinement? and what will those poor women do over yonder with not a single masculine soul to turn to in their helplessness? Not that they wish my help, of course, but I had meant to offer it to them all the same if there was anything I could have done," he added, grimly, to his own self.

The three days dragged away very drearily. On the fourth day Howard availed himself of the aid of a crutch and got into the little public room of the hotel.

Among the few idlers that were gathered about in little friendly groups, he saw a rather intelligent-looking fisherman going from one to another with a small slip of paper in his hand.

As they read it some shook their heads, and some dived into their pockets and brought forth a few pence, which they dropped into the fisherman's extended palm.

Howard was quite curious by the time his turn came. He took the paper in his hand and found it to be an humble petition for charity, which duly set forth:

"WHEREAS, an unknown woman lies ill of a fever at a house of one Fanchette Videlet, a poor widow, almost without the necessaries of life, it is here begged by the said widow that all Christian souls will contribute a mite to the end of securing medical attendance and comforts for the poor unknown wayfarer."

This petition, which was written in excellent French, and duly signed Fanchette Videlet, had a strange effect upon Howard Templeton. His face grew pale as death; his eyes stared at the poor fisherman in perplexed thought, while he absently plunged his hand into his pocket and drew it out full of gold pieces.

CHAPTER XIX.

"Here, my man, take this," he said, putting the coins into the man's hand.

"Why, this is too much, sir," said the honest fisherman, holding his hand out and looking at the gold in surprise. "You will rob yourself, sir."

"No, no; keep it. It is but a trifle," said Howard, pushing his hand back. "But, pray, will you answer a few questions for me?"

"As many as you like, sir—and thank you for your generosity," answered the fisherman, politely.

"I am very much interested in the sad story written here," said Howard, glancing at the paper which he still held in his hand.

"Yes, sir, it is very sad," assented the fisherman.

"How came this unknown sick woman at the Widow Videlet's house?" inquired Howard.

"The poor soul came there a few days ago, sir. She was ill and quite out of her head—could give no account of herself."

"Can you tell me what day she came there?"

"This makes the fourth day since she came, sir. I remember it was the same day you were brought to the hotel."

The young man started. It was the same day that Lora Carroll had disappeared.

Could it be Lora? Had it been some other waif the great sea had cast up from its deep?

"Did you see this woman? Could you describe her to me?" asked Howard, eagerly.

"I saw her the day she came wandering into Dame Videlet's cottage," was the answer.

"You can tell me how she looked then," said Howard, restraining his impatience by a great effort.

"Yes, sir. She was a mere girl in appearance—very young and very beautiful, with black eyes and long, black hair. She was thinly clad in a fine night-dress," answered the fisherman.

"Did you say she was out of her mind?" asked Howard.

"Yes, sir; she raved continually."

"What form did her delirium take?"

"Oh, sir," cried the fisherman, in a tone of pity and sympathy for the wretched unknown, "it seemed like she had lost her baby. She was going around from one to the other in the place asking, asking everyone, for her baby. She said she was so tired and she had lost it out of her arms in the rain and the darkness, and could not find it again."

Howard's heart gave a great, tumultuous bound of surprise, then almost stopped beating with the suddenness of the shock.

It all rushed over him with the suddenness of a revelation.

It had seemed so strange to him that Mrs. St. John should have taken the tender little babe with her in the rain and wind when she went to search for Lora.

The truth flashed over him like lightning now.

Xenie had found the babe upon the sand where Lora had dropped it in her fevered flight.

No wonder she had been so angry and defiant when he had questioned her about it.

He felt sure now, beyond the shadow of a doubt, that the unknown sick woman in the poor widow's cottage could be none other than Lora herself.

"Poor, unhappy creature," he thought, with a thrill of commiseration. "It must be that God himself has sent me here to succor and befriend her."

He rose hurriedly and took up his crutch.

"How far is Dame Videlet's cottage from here?" he inquired.

"But a few rods, sir—a little further on toward the beach," said the fisherman, regarding him in some surprise.

"I will go down there and see that unfortunate woman, if you will guide me," said Howard. "I believe that she is a friend of mine. You may return their pence to those poor fishermen, who can ill spare it, perhaps. I will charge myself with her expenses even if she should not prove to be the person I think she is."

The fisherman looked at him admiringly and hastened to do his bidding.

Then they walked along to the widow's cottage very slowly, for Howard found himself exceedingly awkward in the use of his crutch.

But after all it seemed but a very few minutes before they stood in the one poor little room of Dame Videlet's dilapidated cot bowing to the kind old soul who had taken the poor wayfarer in beneath the shelter of her lowly roof, shared her simple crust with her, and tended her with kindly, Christian hands.

"How is your patient to-day, my kind woman?" inquired the young man.

"Ah, sir, ah, sir, you may even see for yourself," she answered sadly, as she turned toward the bed.

Howard went forward with a quickened heart-beat, and stood by her side looking down at the sufferer.

Yes there she lay—poor little Lora—with wide, unrecognizing, black eyes, with cheeks crimson with fever and parted lips through which the breath came pantingly. A heavy sigh broke unconsciously from Howard's lips.

"Good sir, do you know her?" asked the woman, regarding him anxiously.

"Yes, I know her," he answered; "she is a friend of mine and has wandered away from her home in the delirium of fever. You shall be richly rewarded for your noble care of her."

"I ask no reward but the blessing of Heaven, sir," said the good old woman, piously; "I have done the best I could for her ever since she staggered into the door and asked me for her lost baby."

As if the word struck some sensitive chord in her consciousness, Lora turned her wild, bright eyes upon Howard's face, and murmured in a pathetic whisper:

"Have you found my baby—Jack's baby and mine?"

Alas for Xenie's secret, guarded with such patient care and sleepless vigilance.

Howard looked down upon her with a mist of tears before his sight—she looked so fair, and young, and sorrowful, lying there calling for her lost little child.

"I have lost my baby, I have lost my baby!" she wailed aloud, throwing her arms wildly over her head and tangling her fingers in the long, dark tresses floating over the pillow in their beautiful luxuriance. "It is lost, lost, lost, my darling little one! It will perish in the rain and the cold!"

Involuntarily Howard reached out and took one of the restless white hands in his, and held it in a firm and tender clasp.

"Lora, Lora," he said, in a gentle, persuasive voice, "listen to me. The baby is *found.* Xenie found it on the shore where you lost it out of your arms. It is safe—it is well, with Xenie."

Lora turned her hollow glance upon his face, and though no gleam of recognition shone in her eyes, his impressive words penetrated her soul. She threw out her arms yearningly.

"It is found, it is found! Oh, thank God!" she murmured, happily. "Bring him to me, for the love of Heaven! Lay him here upon my breast, my precious little son!"

"Oh, sir, then it is true she had a child; and it is living. I thought perhaps it was dead," said the poor widow.

"She has a child, indeed, and she lost it in her delirious flight; but her sister found it soon afterward. It is at this moment not more than four miles from here," answered the young man, without reflecting that many things might have happened during his long imprisonment of four days in the lonely little fishing village.

"Then, if you will take my advice, sir, as she is a friend of yours, you will try to get that child here as soon as possible. I will do the best I can for her, and the doctor has promised to do all in his power; but I believe that the child is the only thing that will save her life," said Dame Videlet, gravely shaking her head in its homely white cap.

"It shall be brought," said Howard, earnestly, and without a doubt but that he could keep the promise thus made.

Dame Videlet thanked God aloud, then added that the sooner it were brought the better it would be for the mother.

All the while poor Lora lay tossing in restless pain, and begging piteously for her little child to be laid upon her breast.

Howard bent over her as tenderly and gently as a brother.

"Lora, my poor child, try to be patient," he said. "I will bring the child to you; only be patient a little while."

But it was all in vain to preach patience to that racked heart and weary, fevered brain.

He stole away, followed by despairing cries for the little child—cries that echoed in his heart and brain many days afterward, when his warm heart was half-broken because he could not keep the promise he had made in such perfect confidence and hope.

"How shall I get back to the village four miles away from here?" he asked of the man who had accompanied him and was still waiting for him.

"I can take you in my fishing-boat and row you there, and welcome, sir," was the hearty response. "It's a wee bit leaky, but as good as any other craft about, and there's no conveyance to be had by land."

"What a great simpleton I have been, by George, never to have thought of a boat before," said Howard, looking vexed at himself. "Here I have been four days, and wanting to get back to the village badly, and never thought of all the little boats and the great, wide ocean."

"Mayhap it's all for the best, sir," said the fisherman. "If you had gone back sooner, you might never have found the sick lady, your friend. You should see the hand of the Lord in it, my young sir."

"It looks like it," admitted Howard, "though, truth to tell, *mon ami*, I do not usually look for such intervention in my affairs. His Satanic Majesty is at present controlling my mundane affairs."

"The Lord rules, sir," answered the man, launching his little boat, and trying to make a comfortable and dry seat for his crippled young passenger.

The little boat shot out into the blue and sparkling waves, and danced along like a thing of life in the beautiful spring sunshine.

"We must go a mile below the village to the home of my friend's mother," Howard explained, as they went along.

Then he fell to wondering how Xenie would receive him when he came to her with the glad tidings of Lora's discovery.

"How strange that I should carry *her glad* tidings," he thought. "I am afraid I do not keep to the letter of my vow of hatred as firmly as she does. Would *she* bring me good news as willingly?"

His heart answered no.

The keel grated on the shore, and springing out, they went up to the pretty cottage were Mrs. Carroll had lived in strict retirement for several months with her two daughters.

But there a terrible disappointment awaited Howard.

The cottage was untenanted.

They knocked several times, eliciting no response, and finally opening the doors, they found that the occupants had moved out.

All was still and silent, and Howard's heart sank heavily as he thought of poor Lora lying in the widow's cot and moaning for the child he had promised to bring her.

"They are gone away," said Howard in a more hopeless voice than he knew himself. "We must return to the village. We may hear news from them there."

And in his heart he was fervently praying that he would, for how could he return to Lora without the child?

They went to the little village where the dead body had been washed upon the sands, and he asked everyone he met if they knew where the occupants of the little cottage had gone.

No one could tell him anything of their whereabouts. They had identified the drowned woman as their relative, had buried her, and then quietly left the place, taking Ninon, the little maid, with them.

He could not obtain the least clew by which he might follow them and bring them back to the sick girl whom they mourned as dead.

Howard did not know what to do now, for he remembered that Dame Videlet had said that the child was the only thing that could save Lora's life.

He went into the churchyard and looked at the new-made grave with the cross of white marble, and the simple inscription "Lora, *ætat* 18."

"Perhaps the inscription might come true after all in a few—a very few days," he thought, sadly.

CHAPTER XX.

Howard did not know what to do: it seemed such a terrible thing to go back to Lora with bad tidings. Perhaps the shock would kill her.

Oh, if Mrs. St. John had but waited a little longer! Why need she have hurried away so precipitately?

Well, there was no help for it.

He must go back and tell her how inopportunely things had turned out, and how sorry he was that he could not keep his promise.

He would get Dame Videlet to break it to her very gently.

She would not bungle over it like a great, awkward fellow like himself.

The good old woman was waiting for him outside the door.

Her face was radiant, but it changed and grew very anxious as he came up to her, and she saw that his arms were empty.

"Where is the child?" she whispered.

Briefly and sadly he told the story of his disappointment, and the widow wiped the tears of sorrow from her eyes as he concluded.

"How is she now?" he inquired, anxiously.

"She has been better, much better, since you told her the child was found. Her reason has returned to her, and she has wept tears of joy. She is impatiently waiting for you now, for I told her just now that you were returning. Alas, alas!" groaned Dame Videlet, her tender heart quite melted by the thought of Lora's disappointment.

Howard groaned in unison with her.

"Will it go hard with her?" he asked, sorrowfully.

The dame shook her head mournfully.

"Alas, alas!" she groaned again.

"You will break the news to her—will you not?" asked Howard. "It would be better for you to do it; I am a great, awkward fellow, and could not tell her tenderly and gently like a woman. Tell her we will try to find her mother and sister as soon as possible. Do not let her despair."

"I will tell her," said the good woman, turning toward the door, "but I am afraid the disappointment will nearly kill her. She is very ill. She cannot bear much. Do you remain outside while I go in."

Howard sat down on a rough bench outside the door and waited, his heart heavy with grief for the poor, unfortunate girl within.

"Far better that I had not seen her at all, than have given her such hope only to be followed by disappointment," he thought sadly to himself.

Suddenly a wild, piercing, delirious shriek issued from the widow's cot, causing him to spring up in alarm, and rush into the room.

He met the bereaved mother in the center of the floor, trying to make her escape from the feeble arms of Dame Videlet who was drawing her back to the bed.

She looked like a mad creature struggling with the weak, old woman, her dark hair flying loose in wild confusion, her arms flung upward over her head, while shriek after shriek burst from her foam-flecked lips.

"Take her," cried the old woman, excitedly. "Hold her tightly in your arms a minute."

Howard obeyed her quickly, and in his strong, yet gentle clasp, the mad girl was held securely while Dame Videlet poured something from a bottle upon a sponge and held it to the girl's dilated nostrils.

Directly her wild cries grew fainter, her eyelids fell, her head dropped heavily upon Howard's breast.

"Lay her down upon the bed, now, sir," said the dame, "and fetch the doctor as quickly as you can. This delirium will soon return upon her. The effect of the drug will not last very long."

"She cannot live the night out," said the doctor, sadly.

Three weary days and nights had Lora been tossing restlessly in the delirium of fever. Everything that money or skill could do had been done for her, but all to no avail.

Now, as they stood around the bed and listened to her wild, delirious ravings, the kind old doctor shook his head and sighed at the sight of so much youth and beauty going down to the grave.

"She cannot live the night out," he said again, in a voice of deep feeling.

"Can nothing more be done?" asked Howard Templeton, his blue eyes resting sadly on the wreck of the beautiful Lora.

"I have done all that the medical art can do," declared the physician, "but all to no avail. She has sustained a terrible shock. Her dreadful tramp through the wind and rain the day she came here was enough to have killed her. But her constitution was a superb one, and I believed that I might have saved her after all, if the child could have been restored to her."

"Why did we not think of procuring a substitute for the child?" exclaimed Howard, suddenly. "If we could have put another child in its place might not the innocent deception have saved her life?"

"Such a plan might have been tried," said the doctor, thoughtfully. "But it must have been a terrible risk to tell her the truth even after her recovery. She is very nervous, and her organization is high-strung."

Even as he spoke, the grayness and pallor of death settled over Lora's beautiful, wasted features.

CHAPTER XXI.

"My love, you are simply perfect. You look like a bride."

Mrs. Carroll spoke enthusiastically, and her daughter flushed brightly with gratified pride and pleasure.

She was standing before the long cheval-glass in her dressing-room. She was about to attend a ball at Mrs. Egerton's, and her maid had just put the finishing touches to her toilet.

It was no wonder that Mrs. Carroll's admiration had broken out into enthusiastic words. Xenie's loveliness was dazzling, her toilet perfection.

She wore a dress of the rarest and costliest cream-white lace over a robe of cream-colored satin. The frosty network of the over-dress was looped here and there with diamond stars.

A necklace of diamonds was clasped around her white throat, a diamond star twinkled in the dark waves of her luxuriant hair, and the same rich jewels shone on her breast and at her tiny, shell-like ears.

Her dark and brilliant beauty shone forth regally from the costly setting.

Her eyes outrivaled the diamonds, her satin skin was as creamily fair as her satin robe, her scarlet lips were like rosebuds touched with dew.

No wonder that Mrs. Carroll caught her breath in a kind of ecstacy at the resplendent vision.

More than a year had passed since that dark and rainy morn on the shores of France, when Xenie had wandered up and down on the "sea-beat shore" seeking her lost sister—a year that had brought its inevitable changes, and dulled the first sharp edge of grief—so that to-night she was to throw off her mourning robes and reappear in society for the first time at a ball given by her aunt, Mrs. Egerton.

Yet, after that first moment of exultant triumph at her mother's praise, a faint, intangible shadow settled over Mrs. St. John's brilliant face.

The scarlet lips took a graver curve upon their honeyed sweetness, the dark, curling lashes drooped low, until they shaded the peachy cheek.

The white-gloved hand that held the rare bouquet drooped wearily at her side.

"Mamma," she said, abruptly, "I wish I had not promised to go."

"What has come over you, Xenie? I thought you had looked forward to this night with real pleasure."

"I did—I do, mamma, and yet for the moment my heart grew sad. I was thinking of poor little Lora."

A hot tear splashed down upon her cheek, and Mrs. Carroll sighed heavily, while her grave, sad face grew sadder and graver still. She put her hand upon her heart.

"Oh, that we might have her back!" she breathed, in a voice that was almost a moan of pain.

"The carriage is waiting, madam," said Finette, appearing at the door.

"Well, I am ready," said Mrs. St. John, listlessly. "My cloak, Finette."

The maid came forward and threw the elegant wrap about her shoulders, and leaving a light kiss on her mother's lips, Mrs. St. John swept out of the dressing-room and down to the carriage that waited to take her to the brilliant *fete* that Mrs. Egerton had planned in her especial honor.

Mrs. Carroll bent her steps to the nursery.

Ninon, the little French nurse, sat beside the hearth sewing on a bit of fancy work, and the soft glow of firelight and gaslight shining upon her made her look like a quaint, pretty picture in her neat costume and dark prettiness.

The nursery was a dainty, airy, white-hung chamber. It had been a smoking-room in Mr. St. John's time. His widow had converted it into a nursery.

In a beautiful rosewood, lace-draped crib lay the spurious heir to the millionaire's wealth—a beautiful, rosy healthy boy, sleeping softly and sweetly in innocent unconsciousness of the terrible fraud that had been perpetrated in his name.

For Mrs. St. John's daring scheme had succeeded. Lora's child had been foisted upon the law and the world as the millionaire's legal heir, and Howard Templeton's heritage had passed into the hands of the child's guardian, Mrs. St. John, his pretended mother.

But, alas! in the hour of her triumph, when the golden fruit of her wild revenge was within her grasp, its sweetness had palled upon her, its taste had been bitter to her lips. It was but Dead Sea fruit, after all.

For the struggle with Howard Templeton for the possession of the millionaire's fortune which Xenie had anticipated with such passionate zest had been no struggle after all.

In a few weeks after the burial of the poor drowned woman whom she had identified as her sister, Xenie and her mother had returned to the United States, taking with them Lora's child, and as nurse, Ninon, the little maid-servant.

A costly bribe had sealed the lips of the little French maid, and the truth of the little boy's parentage was a dead secret with her.

Immediately after her arrival at home, Xenie had placed her case in the hand of a noted lawyer.

He undertook it in perfect faith. He did not dream that he had been employed as the necessary aid to carry out a wicked scheme of revenge and perpetrate a gigantic fraud.

He took immediate steps to regain the possession of the deceased millionaire's property in the interest of his posthumous child.

The case immediately attracted public attention and interest, both from the high position of the parties to the suit and the great wealth involved.

But for several months nothing could be heard from the defendant, who was still absent in Europe, although the lawyer who managed his property in his native city wrote him frantic and repeated appeals to return and defend his case.

At length, when patience had ceased to be a virtue with the plaintiff, and the opposition was about to push the suit for judgments without him, a brief letter was received from Howard Templeton, instructing the lawyers to postpone everything until after his arrival.

He would sail on a certain day and upon a certain steamer, and be with them four weeks from date.

Mrs. St. John was quite content to wait after she heard of that letter.

She felt so sure that she would win that she was willing to wait until her enemy came. She wanted to triumph over him face to face.

So the weeks dragged by, and Howard's steamer was due in port.

It did not come. Soon it was a week over-due.

Then came one of those dreadful reports of marine disasters that now and then thrill the great heart of humanity with horror.

There had been a terrible storm at sea, and the ship had gone to pieces upon a hidden rock. Only seven persons had been saved.

Howard Templeton's name appeared in the list of passengers who had perished.

So there could be no further delay now. The case went before the courts and was very speedily decided.

Mrs. St. John gained the case and had her revenge.

But it was no revenge, after all, since Howard Templeton was not alive to pay the bitter cost of her vengeance.

So the golden fruit, bought at the price of her soul's peace, turned to bitter ashes on her loathing lips.

CHAPTER XXII.

"Mrs. St. John, allow me to present to you Lord Dudley."

Xenie turned with a languid smile and bowed to the tall, elegant gentleman who bent admiringly before her.

Only ten minutes before Mrs. Egerton had whispered to her eagerly:

"My dear, Lord Dudley, the great English peer, is present. There's a catch for you."

"I am not looking for a catch," Xenie said, almost bruskly.

"No," said her aunt, who was an indefatigable matchmaker; "but then you are too young and beautiful to remain always single. You are sure to marry some day again, and why not Lord Dudley?"

"He has not asked me, aunt," said Xenie, half-smiling, half-provoked. "I am not even acquainted with him."

"No, but you will be," said Mrs. Egerton. "I heard him asking just now about you. He said you were the most beautiful woman he had ever seen—a compliment worth having from such a man as Lord Dudley, so elegant and distinguished, with such an air of culture and travel. Besides, he is so wealthy, owning several castles in England, I'm told, and a fabulous bank account."

"A distinguished *parti*, certainly," said Xenie, indifferently, and then, as her aunt moved away, she completely forgot Lord Dudley's existence.

She stood leaning carelessly against a tall flower-stand, looking at the dancers, a little later, when Mrs. Egerton approached, leaning on the arm of a handsome gentleman, and then she found herself bowing and smiling in acknowledgement of an introduction to Lord Dudley.

"I have been watching you a long time, Mrs. St. John," he said, taking his place by her side. "Your face puzzled me."

"Indeed?" she said, raising her dark eyes to him with a kind of languid wonder.

"Yes, it is true," he said. Then suddenly, as the intoxicating strains of a waltz began to pulsate on the perfumed air, he exclaimed, in a different tone: "Will you give me this waltz, Mrs. St. John?"

She assented indifferently, and a moment later she was whirling down the long room, the envy of every woman at the ball, for every feminine present had set her cap at the distinguished traveler.

His tall, proud form in the black evening dress showed to the most perfect advantage, as clasping her *petite* and graceful form closely in his arm, they whirled round and round to the enchanting strains, looking, in the perfect accord and gracefulness with which they moved, like the spirit of harmony embodied.

"That will be a match," predicted some of the wiseacres around, and those that did not say that much thought it to themselves.

Among the latter class was a gentleman who had entered a moment before and now stood talking courteously to the hostess.

It was she who had directed his attention to the handsome pair.

"Look at Xenie," she said with a spice of malicious triumph in her tone. "That is Lord Dudley with whom she is waltzing. She has quite captivated him. Doubtless it will be a match."

His eyes followed the flying form a moment steadily, then he answered calmly:

"They are a handsome pair, certainly, Mrs. Egerton. I am acquainted with Lord Dudley."

"You met him abroad, I suppose?"

"No, we came over from England in the same——"

But at that moment someone came hastily up and claimed his attention.

Then a little excited group formed around him, and even the waltzers began to see that an unusual interest was agitating the wall-flowers.

Xenie looked carelessly at first, then more closely as she saw that her aunt stood in the center of the group.

"Aunt Egerton has suddenly become the center of attraction," she said, laughingly, to her companion.

Then she started and the room seemed to swim around her, the lights, the flowers, the black suits of the men, the gay, butterfly robes of the women seemed to be blending in an inextricable maze.

Her heart seemed beating in her ears, so loudly it sounded.

She had caught a flitting glimpse of a man's form standing just beyond her aunt. It was he around whom the excited little throng buzzed and eddied.

He was tall, straight, graceful as a young palm tree, handsome as Apollo, in his elegant evening dress.

His head, crowned with fair, curling locks, was held aloft with half-haughty grace; his Grecian profile, clearly-cut as a cameo head, was turned toward Xenie, and she saw the smile that curved the fair, mustached lips, the flash in the proud, blue eyes.

For a moment she lost the step, and hung droopingly on her partner's arm.

"You are tired," he said, stopping and looking down into her deathly-white face. "Pardon me, I kept you on the floor too long; but your step was so perfect, the music so entrancing, I forgot myself."

He was leading her to a seat as he spoke. She came back to herself with a quick start.

"No, do not blame yourself," she answered. "The fact is I am not accustomed to waltzing of late. This is the first time for almost two years, and it is so easy to—to grow dizzy—to lose one's head."

"Yes, indeed, it is," he answered. "Shall I get you a glass of water?"

"If you please," she murmured, faintly.

He went away, and she tried to rally from her sudden shock.

By the time he returned she was calm, nonchalantly fanning herself with a languid, indolent grace. No one but herself knew how hard and fast her heart was beating yet.

"Thank you," she murmured; then, as she lifted her head, she saw her aunt coming to her, leaning on the arm of a gentleman.

Lord Dudley stared and exclaimed:

"Heaven! it is Howard Templeton! The sea has given up its dead!"

"Do you know him?" asked Xenie.

"Yes, we crossed together. That is—until the terrible storm that wrecked us—I was one of the seven that were saved. It was supposed that Templeton was lost."

"Xenie," said Mrs. Egerton, vivaciously, and yet with a note of warning in her tones that was distinguishable only to her ears for whom it was intended, "here is an old friend whom we all thought dead. Bid him welcome."

Xenie arose, languid, careless, pale as a ghost, yet wearing a gracious smile for the eyes of the little social world that watched her keenly.

He took the half-extended hand in his a moment, and bowed low over it, touching it an instant to his mustached lips.

"I kiss the hand that smites me," he murmured in her ear, sarcastically; then turned aside to greet Lord Dudley.

Fervent congratulations were exchanged between these two, who had been ocean voyagers together, and who had parted on the deck of the broken vessel, expecting to meet again only upon the other shore of eternity.

"I am dying of impatience to hear how you were rescued from the horrors of that terrible shipwreck," said Lord Dudley. "Is the story too long to tell us to-night?"

"It is a long story, but it may be told in a few words," said Howard. "I was tossed about for some time, clinging desperately to a slender spar, then picked up by a blockade runner bound for Cuba.

"This, in turn, was captured by a Spanish war vessel. I remained a prisoner of Spain until such time as the vessel put into port, and I reported to our American consul in that country.

"He immediately wrote to America for the necessary papers to prove my identity as a citizen of America. These being obtained and examined, I was released, after a tedious delay, and came home as fast as wind and tide could carry me. There, my lord, you have the whole story in a nutshell."

"And a very interesting one, too, I doubt not, had it been related in detail. I heartily rejoice that you were saved to tell it," said Lord Dudley, with interest.

Then he added, as if some afterthought had suddenly struck him:

"And, Templeton, the lady—who came over in your care—was she also saved?"

Templeton started, and flashed a hurried glance at Xenie.

She was toying with her jeweled fan, and looking away as carelessly as if she had forgotten his existence.

He did not know that she was listening intently to every word.

He looked back carelessly at the nobleman.

"Yes, she was rescued with me. We clung to the spar together. I would have lost my own life rather than that frail and helpless girl should have perished!"

"She returned with you, then?" said Lord Dudley.

"Yes, she returned in my care. She was a helpless young widow," said Howard, evasively. "She lost all her friends in Europe."

Then other friends claimed him, and he turned away.

"So Mr. Templeton is an old acquaintance of yours, Mrs. St. John?"

"Yes; he was my late husband's nephew," she answered, with languid indifference.

He saw that she did not care to pursue the subject.

"It puzzled me when I first saw you to-night that I could not account for the strange familiarity of your face," he said; "but since I have so unexpectedly met with my fellow-voyager, Howard Templeton, I distinctly recall the reason. You are singularly like a lady who traveled in his care—your very height, your very features; though, as I remember now, very different in expression. She appeared almost heart-broken; yet she was very beautiful. I need not tell you that, though, since I have already said she looks like you," he added, with an admiring bow.

"What was her name?" asked Mrs. St. John, eagerly, quite oblivious of the delicate compliment.

"I have forgotten it," said Lord Dudley. "Forgetting names is a weakness of mine. Yet I remember that Templeton called her by her Christian name—a very soft and sweet one. Let me see—*Laura*, perhaps."

Xenie sat silent and thoughtful. There was a strange pain at her heart. She could not understand it.

"It cannot be that I am sorry he is living," she said to herself. "My triumph is greater than if he were dead. He knows that I have my sweet revenge. It was never sweet until I knew him living to feel its pangs! For all his haughty bearing it must be that he feels it in all its bitterness."

Then a sudden irrelevant thought flashed across these self-congratulations.

"I wonder who that Laura can be? Is he in love with her?"

It was the most natural thought in the world for a woman; yet she put it away from her with a sort of angry impatience.

"What if he does love her?" she thought, scornfully, "He cannot marry her. He is a beggar. I have stripped him of everything. She will leave him for lack of gold, as he left me. Then he may feel something of what I suffered through his sin!"

And she felt gladder than ever before at the thought of Howard Templeton's poverty. She knew that he could not marry the girl for whom he said he would have lost his own life—that beautiful, mysterious *Laura.*

Mrs. Egerton was passing and she called her.

"I am going home," she said. "I have danced too much. I am tired, and the rooms are suffocating."

"A multiplicity of excuses," laughed Lord Dudley. "Ossa upon Pelion piled. Mrs. St. John, you will not be so cruel?"

"I must; my head aches," she replied; and though he pleaded and Mrs. Egerton protested, she was obstinate.

Mrs. Egerton saw her depart, feeling sorely vexed with her.

Howard Templeton saw her leaving, and crossed the room to her.

"I shall do myself the pleasure of calling upon you to-morrow," he said, quietly, as he lightly touched her hand.

They had to wear a mask, these two deadly foes, before the curious eyes of the world.

She flashed a sudden, haughty look of inquiry into his steadfast eyes.

He stooped over her quickly.

"Yes," he whispered, hurriedly and lowly; "it is *vendetta* still. War to the knife!"

Then Lord Dudley, full of regrets, attended her to her carriage.

CHAPTER XXIII.

"Xenie, is that you? Are you just home from the ball?"

Mrs. Carroll turned sleepily on her pillow and looked at the little figure that came gliding in, looking ghost-like in the pale glimmer of the night-lamp in its trailing white robes and unbound hair.

"Yes, mamma, it is I. But I have been home several hours from the ball."

"And not asleep yet, dear?" said Mrs. Carroll, in mild surprise.

"No; I am so restless I cannot sleep. I am sorry I had to disturb you, mamma, but I came to ask you to give me some simple sleeping potion."

"Certainly, love; but wouldn't it be wiser to try and sleep without it? Did you try counting backward?"

She rose as she spoke and turned up the gas. Mrs. St. John laughed—a short, mirthless laugh.

"Oh, yes, mamma, I tried all the usual old-woman remedies, but to no avail. My brain is too excited to yield to trifling measures. Give me something strong that will induce sleep directly."

Her mother, looking at her keenly, saw that she was very pale, and her wide-open, dark eyes looked heavy with some speechless pain.

"Dear, you are not ill, are you?" she inquired, going to a little medicine-case and taking out a small vial and wineglass.

"No, mamma, only nervous and restless. Give me the opiate. It is all I need."

"Did you enjoy the ball?" asked her mother, pouring out the drops with a steady hand. "Who was there?"

"Oh, a number of people. Lord Dudley, for instance. You remember we visited his castle while we were abroad—that great show-place down in Cornwall. I did not tell him about it, though. He is very handsome and elegant. Aunt Egerton recommended him to me as a most desireable catch."

She wanted to tell her mother that the sea had given up its dead—that she had seen Howard Templeton alive and in the flesh, but somehow she could not bring herself to utter his name; so she had rattled on at random.

"Humph! I should think Mrs. Egerton had had enough of making matches for you," her mother muttered. "After the way Howard Templeton treated you she——"

"Oh, mamma," said Xenie, interrupting her suddenly.

"What?" said Mrs. Carroll.

"He—he is here," said Xenie, with a gasp.

"He—who, child?" asked her mother.

"The man you named," said Xenie, in a low voice, as she took the wineglass into her shaking hand.

"Not Howard Templeton?" said Mrs. Carroll, with such an air of blank astonishment that she looked almost ludicrous in her wide-frilled, white night-cap, and Xenie must have laughed if it had not been for that strange and heavy aching at her heart. As it was, she simply said:

"Yes, mamma."

"Then he wasn't shipwrecked, after all—I mean he wasn't drowned, after all. Somebody saved him, didn't they?" said Mrs. Carroll, in a good deal of astonishment.

And again Xenie said, quietly:

"Yes, mamma."

"But how did it all happen? Or did you ask him?" inquired her mother, curiously.

"He is coming here to-morrow. I dare say he will tell you all about it. I am going now. Good-night," said Xenie, draining the contents of the wineglass and setting it down.

"Good-night, my darling," said Mrs. Carroll, looking after her a little disappointedly as she went slowly from the room.

But Xenie did not look back, though she knew that her mother was burning with curiosity to know more of her meeting with Howard Templeton.

She went to her luxurious room, crept shiveringly beneath the satin counterpane, and was soon lost to all mundane interest in the deep sleep induced by the drug she had taken.

She slept long and uninterruptedly, and it was far into the day when she awoke and found her maid, Finette, waiting patiently to dress her.

"You must arrange my hair very carefully, Finette," she said, as the maid brushed out the dark luxuriance of her tresses, "and put on my handsomest morning-dress. I expect a caller this morning."

It always pleased her to appear at her very fairest in Howard Templeton's presence.

She liked for him to realize all he had lost when he gave her back her troth because she was poor, and because he was not manly enough to dare the ills of poverty for her sake.

So Finette arranged the silky, shining, dark hair in a soft mass of waves and puffs that did not look too elaborate for a morning toilet, and yet was exquisitely becoming, while it gave a certain proud stateliness to the *petite* figure.

Then she added a little comb of frosted silver, and laid out several morning-dresses of various hues and styles for the inspection of her mistress.

Mrs. St. John looked them over very critically.

It was a spring morning, but the genial airs of that balmy season had not yet made their appearance sufficiently for an indulgence in the crisp muslin robes that suited the month, so Xenie selected a morning-robe of pale-pink cashmere, richly trimmed in quilted satin and yellowish Languedoc lace.

The soft, rich color atoned for the unusual absence of tinting in the oval fairness of her face, and when she descended to the drawing-room she had never looked lovelier.

The slight air of restless expectancy about her was not enough to detract from her beauty, though it robbed her of repose.

"Mamma, has little Jack come in yet from his morning airing?" she inquired of Mrs. Carroll, who was sorting some bright-colored wools on a sofa.

"Yes, half an hour ago. You slept late," said Mrs. Carroll.

"Let us have him in to amuse us," said Mrs. St. John, restlessly.

Mrs. Carroll rang a bell and a servant appeared.

"Tell Ninon to bring my son here," said Mrs. St. John.

Presently the little French maid appeared, leading the beautiful, richly-dressed child by the hand.

Little Jack rushed forward tumultuously and climbed into Xenie's lap. She kissed him fondly but carefully, taking care that he did not disarrange her hair or dress.

"Pretty mamma," whispered the dark-eyed child, patting her pale cheeks with his dimpled, white hand.

Mrs. St. John smiled proudly, and just then her mother said, with the air of one who vaguely recalls something:

"Did I dream it last night, Xenie, or did you tell me that Mr. Templeton is alive, and that he is coming here to-day?"

There came a sudden hurried peal at the door-bell. Xenie started, growing white and red by turns.

"I told you so," she answered. "And there he is now, I suppose."

She sat very still and waited, clasping the beautiful boy to her wildly beating heart.

There was a bustle in the hall, then the door was thrown open and a gentleman was ushered in.

He was a large, handsome young man, in the uniform of a sea captain. He wore a large, dark beard, and his brown eyes flashed their eagle gaze around the room, half-anxiously, half-defiantly, until they rested on Mrs. St. John's face where she sat clasping the child in her arms.

As she met his gaze she put the child down upon the floor and started up with a low cry.

"*Jack Mainwaring!*" she gasped.

CHAPTER XXIV.

Jack Mainwaring—for it was indeed himself—looked at his sister-in-law with a half-sarcastic smile.

He had no love for Lora's relations. He considered that they had treated him badly. He was as well-born as they were, and had been better off until Xenie had married the old millionaire.

Yet they had flouted his love for Lora and refused to sanction an engagement between them, hoping to send her to the city and find a richer market for her beauty. So it was with a smile of scorn he contemplated the agitation of the beautiful young widow.

"Yes, Mrs. St. John, it is Jack Mainwaring," he said, grimly. "Don't be alarmed, I won't eat you."

Xenie regarded him with a stare of haughty amazement.

"I do not apprehend such a calamity," she said, icily. "But—I thought you dead."

"Yes," he said. "I have passed through some terrible disasters, but luckily I escaped with my life. You will not care to hear about that, though, so I will not digress. I will say that I came up from the country this morning. I went down there yesterday to look for Lora. You will wonder, perhaps, why I am here this morning."

Mrs. Carroll had sent the nurse away as soon as he entered. They were alone, she and Xenie and the child, with the handsome, desperate young man, looking as if he hovered on the verge of madness.

He had not even spoken to his mother-in-law, who regarded him with a species of terror.

Xenie fell back into her seat at the mention of Lora's name. Her lip quivered and her eyes filled.

"You—you surely have not come for Lora," she said, and her voice was almost a moan of pain. "You surely must have heard——"

"That *my wife* is dead," he said, and his voice shook so that it was scarcely audible. "Yes, they told me she was drowned. Is it true?"

"She—she drowned herself," answered Xenie, in a low tone of passionate despair.

She had not asked him to sit down, but Captain Mainwaring dropped down heavily into a chair with a groan of mortal agony, and hid his convulsed face in his hands.

"Oh, my God, *no*!" he cried out, wildly. "They did not tell me that. It is not true. It cannot be true. She would not have done that, my little Lora!"

"It is all your fault," cried out Mrs. Carroll, confronting him with a pale face and flashing eyes. "You drove her to it, Jack Mainwaring, you broke her heart. You killed her as surely as if your hand had pushed her into that great, cruel sea where she found her death!"

"She was my wife—I loved her," said the sailor in a voice of anguish, as he lifted his wet eyes to the face of the angry mother of his lost one. "*You* were the cruel one. You denied her my love, and perhaps when you found out that she belonged to me in spite of you, you tormented her to death."

Mrs. Carroll did not answer him. She was afraid to speak. A moment ago, in her rage and excitement, words had hovered on her lips that would have betrayed the fact that a child had been born to Lora.

But a quick telegraphic signal from her daughter arrested the truth on her lips. So she remained silent, fearful that some angry, unguarded word might betray Xenie's perilous secret.

Meanwhile little Jack clung to Mrs. St. John's dress, and regarded the big, handsome, bearded seaman with fearless, fascinated eyes.

The door opened suddenly and Howard Templeton stepped into the room, but no one saw him or heard him, so intense was the excitement that pervaded their hearts.

He was about to advance toward Mrs. Carroll when he saw Jack Mainwaring sitting in a position that screened the new-comer from the ladies, while it exposed to full view his own anguished and tear-wet face.

Howard paused instantly and stared at the handsome sailor with increasing surprise each moment, until that expression was succeeded by one of fervent pleasure.

He had known Jack Mainwaring quite well several years before, and had been sincerely sorry when he had heard of his loss at sea.

Now, after one puzzled moment, resulting from Jack's long, glossy beard, he recognized him, and his heart leaped with joy to think that Lora's husband was still numbered among the living.

"But I did not come here to bandy words," continued poor Jack, lifting his bowed head dejectedly. "Mrs. St. John, will you tell me how long my wife has been dead?"

Xenie named the date in a half-choked voice. It was fourteen months before.

Captain Mainwaring took a well-worn letter from his pocket and ran over it again, while his manly face worked convulsively with emotion; then he said, in a voice that quivered with deep feeling:

"My poor Lora, my unfortunate wife, left me a child, then. Where is that child, Mrs. St. John?"

A blank, terrified silence overwhelmed the two women. Instinctively Xenie's arm crept around the child at her knee and drew him closer to her side.

Captain Mainwaring had scarcely noticed little Jack before, but Xenie's peculiar action attracted his attention. He rose and took a step toward her.

"You do not answer me," he said. "Can it be, then, that this is Lora's child and mine?"

Xenie caught the child up and held him tightly to her breast, while she faced the speaker with wild, angry eyes, like a lioness at bay.

"Back, back!" she cried, "do not touch him! This is *my* child—mine, do you hear? How dare you claim him?"

"Yours, yours," cried the sailor, retreating before the passionate vehemence of her voice and gestures; "I—I did not know you had a child, madam."

"You did not," cried Xenie with breathless defiance. "No matter. Ask mamma, there. Ask Doctor Shirley! Ask anyone you choose. They will all tell you that this is my child—*my* child, do you understand?"

"Madam, I am not disputing your word," cried poor Jack, in amaze at her angry vehemence. "Of course you know best whose child it is. But will you tell me what became of Lora's baby?"

Mrs. St. John stared at him silently a moment, then she answered, coldly:

"Lora's baby? Are you mad, Jack Mainwaring? Who told you that she had a baby?"

His answer was a startling one:

"Lora told me so herself, Mrs. St. John."

Xenie St. John reeled backward a few steps, and stared at the speaker with parted lips from which every vestige of color had retreated, leaving them pallid and bloodless as a ghost's.

"What, under Heaven, do you mean?" she inquired, in a hollow voice.

Captain Mainwaring held up the letter in his hand.

"Do you see this letter?" he said. "It is the last one Lora wrote me. I received it at the last port we touched before our ship was burned. She begged me to come back to her at once if I could, and save her name from the shadow of disgrace. She told me that a child was coming to us in the spring. I—oh, God, I was frantic! I meant to return on the first homeward bound vessel! Then came the terrible fire and loss of the vessel. Days and days we floated on a raft—myself and three others—then we were rescued by a merchant vessel bound for China. We had to go there before we could come home. For months and months I endured inconceivable tortures thinking of my poor young wife's terrible strait. And after all—when I thought I should so soon be at home and kiss her tears away—I find her *dead*!"

His voice broke, he buried his face in his hands, and, strong man though he was, sobbed aloud like a child.

They watched him, those four—Templeton, himself unseen—the frightened mother and daughter, and the little child with its sweet lips puckered grievingly at the man's loud sobs.

But in a minute the man mastered himself, and went on sadly:

"I was half frantic when I heard that my wife was dead. But, after awhile, I remembered the little child. I said to myself, I will go and seek it. If it be a little girl I will call it Lora. It may comfort me a little for its mother's loss."

He paused a moment, and looked at the pale, statue-like woman before him.

"Where is the child?" he asked, almost plaintively.

Her eyes fell before his earnest gaze, her cheeks blanched to the pallor of marble.

"She must have been mistaken," she faltered. "There was no child."

The young sailor regarded her keenly.

"Madam, I do not believe you," he answered, bluntly. "You are trying to deceive me. I ask you again, where is my child? Is it dead? Was it drowned with its hapless young mother?'"

"I tell you there was no child," she answered, defiantly, stung to bitterest anger by his words.

"But there *was* a child," persisted Captain Mainwaring. "Lora would not have deceived me."

"Not willfully, I know, but she was mistaken, I tell you," was the passionate response.

"I do not believe you, Mrs. St. John. You are trying to deceive me for some purpose of your own. You kept my wife from me, and you would fain keep my child, also. You have hidden it away from me! Nay, I believe on my soul that it is my child you hold in your arms and claim as your own. Give it to me," he cried, advancing upon her.

But she retreated from him in terror.

"Never! never!" she cried out, in a passionate voice.

"Xenie, Xenie!" cried Howard Templeton, advancing sternly, "do not stain your soul longer with such a horrible falsehood. Give Jack Mainwaring the child! You well know that it is his and Lora's own!"

CHAPTER XXV.

Xenie St. John turned with a half-stifled shriek and looked at the daring intruder.

She saw her enemy standing in the center of the room looking down at her from his princely hight with a lightning flash of scorn in his bright blue eyes, his lips set sternly under his curling blonde mustache.

He was elegantly attired in the most fashionable morning costume, and his fair, proud Saxon beauty had never appeared more striking. Xenie's dark eyes flashed their gaze into his blue ones with a blaze of passionate defiance.

"How dare you say so?" she cried, stamping her small, slippered foot upon the rich carpet with angry vehemence. "Are you mad, Howard Templeton?"

He stood still, folding his arms across his broad breast, regarding her with a steady calmness strangely at variance with her passionate vehemence.

"No, I am not mad," he answered, in low, even tones, while his blue eyes gazed strangely into her own—"I am not mad, and I dare assert nothing but what I know to be the truth. So I repeat what I said to you just now. Give Captain Mainwaring the innocent little child in whose name you have perpetrated such a monstrous fraud. It is his child and your sister's. I will prove it, and swear to it if necessary, before any court in the land."

The calm and steady assurance of his words and looks and tones struck Xenie with inward terror. Yet it seemed to her impossible that Howard Templeton could really know the truth. Her heart quaked with terror, yet she tried to brave it out in very desperation.

"How dare you say so?" she repeated, but her voice faltered, and she trembled so that she could scarcely hold the little child in her arms.

Mrs. Carroll crept to her side and stood there dumbly, filled with a yearning desire to help Xenie and shield her from the consequences of her sin, but so horror-stricken that she could not even speak.

Howard Templeton regarded Xenie with a look of scornful amazement.

"Madam," he said, in clear, ringing, vibrant tones, "I can scarce believe that you will try to persist in this terrible deception in the face of all that I have said. Listen, then, and you shall know why I dare confront you with your sin."

"Speak on," she answered, cresting her beautiful head so defiantly, and looking at him so proudly that no one, not even her mother, dreamed of the terrible pain that ached at her heart.

"I have known of this deception from the first," he said. "Ever since the evening I called upon your sister, before you went to Europe. You personated Lora very cleverly. I will give you that much credit; but you did not deceive me five minutes. I saw through the mask directly, and understood the daring game you were playing in furtherance of your revenge against me. Your clever acting did not blind me. I had loved you once, remember, and the eyes of love are very keen."

Alternately flushing and paling, Xenie stared at him, still clasping the little child to her wildly beating heart.

"Bah!" she cried out, contemptuously, as he paused; "who would believe this wild tale that you are telling? If you suspected me, why did you not speak out?"

"I had a fancy to see the farce played out," he answered, coldly. "I was curious to know how far you would willfully wander in the path of sin to gratify your thirst for revenge. I followed you to Europe, although you did not dream of such a thing until that wild and rainy dawn when you met me on the shore near your cottage."

A groan forced itself though her pallid lips as she recalled that dreadful day.

"But, Xenie," he continued, slowly, "I never meant to let matters go as far as they have gone. It amused me for a little while to watch your desperate game, but I always intended to check you before you consummated your clever plan. But that strange power that some call fate, and others Providence, has come between me and my first intention. You have tasted the full sweetness of the cup of revenge, and now you are doomed to drink the bitter dregs. The disgraceful truth will all be known. The wealth you have cheated me of by a terrible fraud will have to be restored. The time has come when I cannot spare you if I would."

She shivered as if an icy wind had blown against her, so impressive were his looks and words; but she saw that Captain Mainwaring was looking at her with mingled wrath and scorn on his handsome, honest face; and the spirit of defiance only grew stronger within her.

"I defy you," she began, imperiously, but the words died half-uttered on her lips, and a shriek of fear and terror burst forth instead.

For the closed door had opened silently and suddenly, and a beautiful, fragile-looking woman had glided into the room.

Xenie thought it was the ghost of her who lay in that green grave under the skies of France, with the white cross marked: "Lora, ætat 18."

The beautiful intruder paused a moment and gazed questioningly around her.

As if by magic, her gaze encountered that of the young sea captain who was staring at her with wild, half-frightened eyes, like one who sees a vision.

Lora—for it was indeed herself—gazed at the handsome young sailor a moment in bewilderment; then a wild and piercing shriek of joy burst from her lips. She rushed forward and threw herself upon his broad breast in a transport of happiness.

"Oh, Jack, Jack!" she cried, twining her white arms tightly around his neck, "you are alive! What happiness for your poor Lora!"

Captain Mainwaring clasped and kissed her with passionate joy, understanding nothing very clearly except the one ecstatic fact that Lora was indeed alive, and having through his deep joy a vague consciousness that Mrs. St. John had somehow terribly wronged and deceived him.

"You see," said Howard Templeton, coldly to Xenie as she stared speechlessly. "Lora has returned to claim her own. Your reign is over."

Lora heard the words, and breaking from the fond clasp of her husband's arms, turned to her sister.

"Oh, Xenie!" she cried, then she stopped short, and her lovely face flushed and her dark eyes beamed.

She had caught sight of the beautiful boy that nestled in the clasp of her sister's arms.

Lora watched him a moment with parted lips and eager eyes.

"Oh!" she breathed, in tones of ineffable tenderness, "how beautiful he is!" then, in low and almost humble accents, she murmured: "Xenie, you will let me kiss him once."

"It is Lora's voice and face," cried Mrs. St. John, half-retreating before her as she advanced, "and yet I saw Lora lying dead—drowned in the cruel sea!"

"No, no," cried Lora, eagerly, "that poor creature you saw drowned was not your sister, Xenie."

"She wore your shawl, your rings," exclaimed Mrs. St. John, incoherently.

"Yes, that is true," said Lora, patiently, "but I can easily explain that, Xenie. She was a poor, mad creature that I met in my wandering—even madder than myself, perhaps, for I remember it all distinctly. She stripped me of my shawl and my jewels—to make herself fine as she said. I let her have them and she went away and left me. Then it must have been that she cast herself into the sea. It was she whom they found and whom you buried under the marble cross with my name upon it. She was some poor, unknown unfortunate whom you mourned as your sister."

She came closer to her sister's side as she spoke, and looked up pleadingly into her face.

"Xenie, you will not disown me, will you? I am indeed your sister, Lora, although you thought me dead. I owe my life to Howard Templeton. He found me ill and dying in a poor woman's cot, and cared for me and saved me. Yes, at the very last hour, when they said I was dying, he would not give me up. He brought a little baby and laid it in my arms, and life came back to me at the touch of the little lips and hands. He deceived me, but it was for my own good. It saved my life, and when I grew stronger I could bear to be told of the innocent deception he had practiced, and I gave back the child to the kind peasant mother who had lent it to me to save my life. But, oh, Xenie, if I talked all day I could never tell you how much I owe to Howard Templeton. He has been all that the best and noblest brother on earth could be! You must not hate him any longer. Xenie, you must forgive him and be kind to him for my sake, since but for his tender care I must surely have died."

As she ceased to speak, Jack Mainwaring strode forward and caught Howard Templeton's hands in a grasp of steel. Words failed him, but the tearful gaze of the honest eyes was far more expressive of his gratitude than the most eloquent speech.

But Xenie remained still and speechless. She suffered Lora to kiss and caress her, but she remained still and pale, seemingly incapable of a return of her sister's tenderness. Her dark eyes stared straight before her, filled with a dumb terror, as if some dread anticipation was painted on the walls of her mind.

Slowly, like one fascinated, Lora crept nearer, and twining her arms about her little child, kissed his sweet brow and lips. Xenie turned mechanically and their eyes met.

They regarded each other silently a moment, but in Lora's eyes there was a yearning tenderness, a plaintive prayer that said plainer than words:

"Oh! my sister, give me my child. Let me lay him in his father's arms, and say: 'My husband, this is my child and yours.'"

The ice around Xenie's frozen heart melted at that wordless prayer. Slowly she laid the beautiful, dark-eyed boy in the yearning arms of the young mother.

"Take him, Lora," she said, "I absolve you from your vow of silence. I cannot withhold this crowning joy that will complete your happiness, although it wrecks my own. Upon my head fall all the bitter consequences of my sin."

With the words she turned to leave the room, but that bitter renunciation before her deadly foe had been too hard for her.

She staggered blindly a moment, then fell to the floor like one bereft of life.

CHAPTER XXVI.

On the deck of a noble steamer outward bound, Lora Mainwaring leaned upon her husband's arm and waved a fond farewell to her mother and sister who watched her tearfully from the shore.

Captain Mainwaring was about to make his first voyage as the commander of the vessel, and his wife chose to go with him, declaring that she feared the dangers of the sea far less than the anguish of a second separation from her husband.

Yet the tears stood thickly in her eyes as she clasped the dimpled hand of her little son and watched those two sad figures on the shore—the beloved mother and sister whom she was leaving for long and weary months—and it might be, for who could tell—perhaps forever!

Two months had passed since the eventful day when Lora had returned to the dear ones who mourned her as dead—two months of passionate happiness to her, yet crowded with bitterness and humiliation to her beautiful and high-spirited sister.

For yet again had the fabulous fortune of the old millionaire changed hands, and Howard Templeton was victor now.

Her passionate revenge, her perilous secret belonged to the world now. It was as Howard had said. He could not have spared her if he would, for Jack Mainwaring was filled with rage and scorn at the knowledge that Xenie had made his innocent child the instrument of a wicked revenge.

Passionate and impulsive, and hating his wife's relations with cordial good will, Jack lost no time in spreading the story to the winds.

The day came when a bitter impulse moved him to repentance, but it was too late to undo his work.

"You were very wrong, Jack," little Lora said to him, tearfully; "you should have remembered that it was not for her sake alone my sister planned and carried out the deception. She gained her revenge, but she also saved my name from obloquy. When you rail so bitterly against her, do not forget that I also lent myself to the deception in my cowardly fear of the world's censure."

So Captain Mainwaring was slowly brought to take a more reasonable view of the case. He apologized bluntly but heartily to Xenie, and she forgave with him an almost apathetic indifference.

For the beautiful and passionate woman was changed now almost beyond belief. Even as she had hastened to be revenged on Howard Templeton for her wrongs, she now made haste to offer restitution. He had no need to contend for his rights. Every dollar of which she had defrauded him was now legally restored to him again.

And when that act of restitution was accomplished, Xenie fell into strange and dangerous apathy. The idle tongues of the world wagged busily, but she of whom they gabbled remained secluded in her beautiful home, silent, thoughtful, sufficient unto herself, heedless alike, it seemed, of their praise or blame.

But the sorrowing mother who daily condemned herself for her share in the trouble, as she anxiously watched her daughter, saw that her delicate cheek was growing thin and white, the brilliant lustre was fading from the mournful black eyes, the musical voice had a subtle tone of weariness. How could it be otherwise when she had lost so much at one fell stroke of fate?

Fortune, revenge, the world's applause, even the little child whom she had loved almost as her own, had slipped from her clasp in an hour, and left her empty-handed on the bleak shores of fate.

She did not know what to do with her blank and ruined life, and her empty heart whose idols all lay shattered in the dust.

So she went her way in silence, not caring to look back, not daring to look forward. For what was left to her now? Nothing but life in a world that seemed to have ended for her forever—life "more pathetic than death."

So, as she turned her dim eyes away from the gallant ship that was bearing Lora so swiftly away from her native land, she said in a voice that was sadder than tears:

"Let us go home, mother."

And while Lora went sailing away over the blue summer sea, beneath the smiling sky of June, they turned their faces homeward.

"Aunt Egerton!"

"Yes, dear," said the elegant woman of fashion, rising with a rustling of silk and lace to greet her niece. "It is I. I came early on purpose to go with you and see little Lora off, but you were already gone. I would have followed you, but they told me I should be too late. So I waited for you here."

Then she rustled back to her seat again and there ensued an embarrassed silence.

For this was the first time that Mrs. Egerton had crossed the threshold since the story of Xenie's revenge and its ultimate failure had become known to the carping world.

She, in common with the world, had been terribly shocked by the disclosure, and had been in full accord with society when it turned its back upon its whilom beautiful favorite.

Now, as she sat there in the rich arm-chair of violet velvet, with all the prestige of her rank and wealth about her, she shrank uneasily before the half-veiled scorn in the beautiful, dusky eyes of the woman who sat opposite regarding her with a cold, inquiring glance.

Turning to her sister-in-law, Mrs. Carroll, she engaged her in a little desultory chat while she recovered her self-possession.

"So Lora has gone on a voyage with her husband?"

"Yes," Mrs. Carroll said, briefly.

She was silently wondering to herself what had brought her proud sister-in-law to Xenie's house after she had, in the world's parlance, so completely "cut" her.

"Is she quite happy?" continued Mrs. Egerton, patronizingly.

She had a private opinion that no one could be happy in such a misalliance as Lora had made, but she forbore to air her secret views for the benefit of her auditors.

"Lora is perfectly happy, I believe," was the confident answer.

"Ah, I am very glad. Her story has been as romantic as a novel. I am pleased to hear that it has ended in the same happy fashion."

Then she turned to Mrs. St. John.

"Xenie, I expect you were surprised to find me here this morning. You must have thought——"

She paused here, a little disconcerted by the steady fire of the proud, dark eyes that gravely regarded her.

"Ah, well," she resumed in a moment, with a little laugh, "I have been sadly vexed with you, Xenie. Who could help it? I had been so proud of you, and hoped such great things for you, I could hardly bear it when I learned to what length your passion had carried you."

She paused in sheer pity as she saw the blush of shame flashing suddenly into those white cheeks.

"Well, never mind," she continued, with a significant smile. "All is not lost yet. We will not recall the past. But I wish to talk to your mother. Won't you gather a bunch of your beautiful roses for me, dear, while we have our little chat?"

Glad of an excuse for leaving the room, Xenie turned away, followed by a smile of blended triumph and cunning from her maneuvering aunt.

She ran down the marble steps at one side of the house that led into the beautiful rose-garden that lay glowing and blushing under the balmy sky of June.

Running down the graveled path, she stopped short very suddenly, and a low cry escaped her lips:

"Howard Templeton!"

CHAPTER XXVII.

A gentleman, standing alone beside a marble fountain, turns with a start and looks at her. His face is handsome, eager, agitated.

"Mrs. St. John," he says; then a strange constraint seems to fall upon both. They remain standing still and regarding each other in painful silence.

It is the first time they have met since the day of her terrible humiliation, more than two months ago. In the passionate war they waged he had been the victor. One would think that he would meet her now with words of exultation.

Yet he is silent, and a dark-red flush creeps slowly up his temples, while his handsome blue eyes regard her with a strange intentness.

To the day of his death he remembers her as she looks now. Not the expression of a feature, not a fold of her robe escapes his memory.

She looks like some beautiful, pale statue.

"Gown'd in pure white that fitted to the shape—A single stream of all her soft, dark curlsPour'd on one side."

The sunshine beams upon her lovingly. A creeping rose-tree throws out its briery arms as though it would fain draw her into its thorny embrace. The light breeze scatters the scented rose-petals in a shower of sweetness under her feet. A happy bird warbles its lay of love above her drooping head.

Suddenly she turns to go, thrilled with a bitter pang of remembrance.

The movement breaks the spell that binds him. He springs after her.

"Do not go," he exclaims, in a voice of unconscious pleading.

"Why should I stay?" she asks, turning her proud, dark eyes upon him. "Why have you intruded your unwelcome presence upon me?"

The flush on his fair, handsome face deepens.

"Xenie, pardon the *ruse* by which I have gained admittance to your presence," he exclaims. "I wished to see you and I went to Mrs. Egerton, and stating my reasons, begged her to arrange this meeting."

"Did you not know that the very sight of you is hateful in my eyes?" she demands, spiritedly.

"I feared so," he answers, with an unconscious tone of sadness in his voice. "Yet I wished to see you. There is something I have to tell you."

"You can tell me nothing that I wish to hear," she retorts, haughtily. "Let me pass, sir. I refuse to listen!"

But the tall, handsome form blocks her way, and shows no signs of yielding.

"Stay, one moment, Xenie," he exclaims. "Suppose I tell you that your vengeance is secure after all—that Uncle John's missing will is found at last?"

She whirls toward him, her dark eyes blazing with incredulous surprise.

"At last!" she says, with a stifled gasp. "At last! And who—who——"

"I found it," he answers, not waiting for her to finish the incoherent question. "He had hidden it, I cannot imagine why, in the most unlikely place in the world. By the merest accident I came upon it yesterday. Take it, Xenie. It secures your revenge to you now, beyond the shadow of a doubt."

He drew an official-looking document from his breast and placed it in her shaking hand. She holds it in a mechanical grasp, her dark, wondering eyes lifted to his proud, agitated face.

"Yes," he repeats, slowly, "your vengeance is now secure. Every penny of my Uncle John's vast wealth is bequeathed to you in the legal document you hold in your hand. I am left utterly penniless!"

But instead of the triumphant joy he expects to see in her mobile face, her look of wonder deepens.

"*You* found the will—*you* brought it to me," she says, with slow gravity. "Who knows of it besides yourself?"

"No one except your aunt, Mrs. Egerton," he answers, calmly; "I have told her, and she is very anxious to congratulate you."

Her red lips curl with faint scorn. But she does not speak. This sudden turn of fortune's wheel seems to have dazed her. She stands quite still holding the precious paper in her tightly-clasped hand, while her dark eyes fix themselves upon it in a strange, intent fashion.

She has lost her revenge, she has lost the world's applause, but this little bit of yellow paper is able to buy it all back for her. It seems too stupendous to believe.

"Why have you done this thing?" she asks, rousing herself, and lifting a curious glance to the silent man before her.

"I do not understand you," he begins, half-haughtily.

"Oh! yes, you do," she interrupts him quickly. "When you found this will, which leaves you penniless, and me, your enemy, triumphant, you must have been tempted to destroy it. You knew that I had resorted to a fraud in order to gain my revenge. How did you conquer the temptation to repay me likewise? Were you nobler than I that you did not burn this paper and keep your uncle's wealth?"

"Xenie, if you will answer me one simple question, I will tell you why I beat down the temptation to keep the wealth which has caused us both so many a bitter heart-ache," he said to her, in a grave, sad voice.

"I will answer you," she repeated, slowly.

"Tell me this, then, Xenie. In the hour when the result of your hopes and plans became known to you—when you thought you had fully secured the revenge for which you had toiled—did your success make you happy?"

"No," she answered, in low but steady tones, while her whole frame quivered with suppressed emotion.

"No," he re-echoed; "revenge has not in it the elements of happiness. It is but a consuming fire that destroys everything sweet and lovely. We both have proved it; therefore, Xenie, I will have no more to do with it. I have repented in bitterness of spirit the deadly feud we waged so long against each other. The only atonement that was left to me you hold in your hand."

"It was a brave atonement when you remember all that it involves for you," she cried, with a sudden remorseful pity in her voice. "You have been nobler than I have."

"Perhaps it was only selfish after all," he answered, impulsively; "for, Xenie, I have been very unhappy in your unhappiness. Every arrow that was pointed at your heart has pierced mine. I have long ago realized that, no matter how terrible the loss to myself, I could never be happy save in the ultimate triumph of the woman I love."

"Love!" she echoed, looking at him with a wondering, startled gaze.

The blue eyes met hers, full of mad, hopeless passion, so long repressed and beaten down that now it seemed a consuming flame.

"Yes, love," he answered, recklessly. "Forgive me, Xenie, but let me speak one moment. Do you think I have forgotten those brief, bright days when we loved each other? Do you think I can ever forget them? I have never ceased to love you; I never shall until this beating heart is dust and ashes! I count that one bright memory of our mutual love worth all its bitter cost!"

The burning crimson flashed into her cheeks. Did he mean it—all that those impetuous words implied?

"You cannot fool me with empty words," she cried. "Do I not know better? Could my love be so much to you when you threw it away for—for this that I hold in my hand?" and she threw a glance of scorn upon the paper in her grasp that represented all the vast wealth of the old millionaire.

There was a moment's silence; then the pent-up heart of the man broke out into passionate words; the bird in the bough overhead hushed its song and seemed to listen.

"Xenie, Xenie, my love and lost darling, why will you wrong me so? Oh, my God! how little I weighed that filthy lucre against your love! I swear to you here, under this blue heaven, and in this hour when I never expect to behold your beautiful face again, that I broke our troth alone because I loved with too dear a passion to doom you to the ills of poverty for my sake. I love you, Xenie, deeply, fondly, devotedly, and I gloried in the thought of lavishing wealth upon you; and when my uncle bade me resign you I gave up my hope—not because I was afraid to brave poverty *for* you, but because I dared not face it *with* you. Darling, how could I bear to doom you, my tender flower, to the ills of poverty and want? But, there, I have told you all this before, and you would not believe it. Why should I weary you again? It is only because I am leaving you forever that I have yielded to the weakness. Farewell, Xenie, and may God bless you!"

He ceased, and in the solitude and stillness of the odorous rose garden it seemed to him as if she must hear his heart beating, so loud and fast were its throbs of anguish. But she was silent, and he turned to go.

"Howard, stay," she murmured, faintly.

He retraced his steps to her side.

"Xenie, what are you doing?" he cried in horror; for she had taken the millionaire's will between her white and jeweled fingers and was tearing it swiftly into the smallest fragments.

The tiny white bits were flying from her hands like a miniature snow-storm.

She laughed lightly at his look of horror.

"John St. John never meant me to have all his money," she answered. "I coerced him into making this will, and he hid it then, hoping, no doubt, that it would never be found. There is an end of it. Let all remain as it was before. You have your share and I mine."

"And your revenge?" he asked, looking at her as if he doubted his own sanity.

"Never speak of it again," she answered, turning from him, while the crimson blush of shame overspread her face.

A wild hope, undreamed of before, darted into his mind. He caught her hand in his.

"Xenie, why have you done this thing?" he asked.

Her dark eyes lifted to his, full of a noble repentance.

"Because I love you," she answered, "and I cannot war against you any longer. Forgive me, Howard; it was never hatred that wrought my sin; it was the cruel madness of love."

He caught her in his arms with a low cry of passionate thanksgiving, and the little birds, listening in the nests above their heads, heard the sound of kisses and passionate words, mixed with a woman's happy sobs.

"Xenie," he said, presently, when her sobs grew calmer, "they told me that Lord Dudley had sued for your hand, and that you had promised to return to England with him as his bride. You cannot imagine what I suffered when I heard it. Even while I thought you hated me I could never feel indifferent to you, though I tried hard to put you out of my heart."

"Lord Dudley asked me," she whispered back. "He was very noble. He knew all my story, but he judged me very gently, and he would have given me his name and love, but I told him it might never be—that I had loved but one in my life, and that I could never love another."

He pressed a dozen kisses on the sweet red lips that whispered the fond confession.

"And you forgive me everything, do you, Howard?" she questioned, gravely. "You know that I have sinned very grievously. I have almost periled my soul in my mad rage for an unholy revenge."

"May God forgive you as freely as I do, my darling," he answered, fondly.

When they strolled into the drawing-room arm-in-arm, a little later, Mrs. Egerton rose from her arm-chair, rustling more than ever in her happy self-importance.

"My dear Xenie," she simpered, "let me be the first to congratulate you that your husband's missing will is found at last."

For answer, Xenie drew her to the window.

"Aunt Egerton, I forgot your bunch of roses," she said, "but I want you to look down there in that graveled walk."

She pointed to the tiny fragments of paper, and Mrs. Egerton's face grew pale.

"What is it?" she asked, uneasily.

"It is St. John's will," Xenie answered steadily, yet crimsoning painfully beneath her aunt's curious glance.

"And you have destroyed it," Mrs. Egerton exclaimed. "Were you mad, child?"

Xenie looked at her aunt with a gesture of proud humility.

"No," she answered, "I have been mad, but, thank God I have come to my senses at last. I destroyed the will because I had wronged Howard enough already without taking his inheritance from him. I have confessed my faults to him and he has forgiven everything."

"And the long vendetta is over," said Mrs. Egerton. "Henceforth you will be——" she paused for a suitable word.

"Xenie will be my wife," said Howard Templeton, drawing near.

Mrs. Carroll, who had been silent all this while, drew near and took her daughter for one moment into the tender clasp of her maternal arms.

"God bless you, my daughter," she murmured. "You have known deep sorrow—may your future years be very happy ones."

My readers, we close our story as we began it—with a wedding. But this time the wedding bells indeed are "golden bells," ringing out the mellow chimes of true happiness.

For this is not the union of winter and summer, this is not the sordid barter of youth and beauty for an old man's gold. It is that one true and beautiful union upon earth where the solemn vow of marriage welds eternally together

"Two souls with but a single thought,Two hearts that beat as one."

CPSIA information can be obtained
at www.ICGtesting.com
Printed in the USA
LVHW052359021121
702257LV00007B/730

9 789355 345622